VGM Opportunities Series

OPPORTUNITIES IN
JOURNALISM
CAREERS

Donald L. Ferguson
Jim Patten

Foreword by
Morley Safer
CBS News

VGM Career Horizons
a division of *NTC Publishing Group*
Lincolnwood, Illinois USA

Cover Photo Credits:
Front cover: upper left, Jeff Ellis, with
permission of the *Chicago Sun Times;* upper
right and lower left, Pioneer Press Newspapers;
lower right: *Chicago Tribune.*

Back cover: upper left and lower right,
Cable News Network, Inc.; upper right,
Pioneer Press Newspapers; lower left,
Jeff Ellis.

Library of Congress Cataloging-in-Publication Data

Ferguson, Donald L.
   Opportunities in journalism careers / Donald L. Ferguson, Jim
Patten

       p.   cm. — (VGM opportunities series)
   1. Journalism—United States—Vocational guidance. I. Patten,
Jim. II. Title. III. Series.
PN4797.F48 1992
071'.3'023—dc20

                                                          91-43518
                                                               CIP

1994 Printing

Published by VGM Career Horizons, a division of NTC Publishing Group.
© 1993 by NTC Publishing Group, 4255 West Touhy Avenue,
Lincolnwood (Chicago), Illinois 60646-1975 U.S.A.
All rights reserved. No part of this book may be reproduced, stored
in a retrieval system, or transmitted in any form or by any means,
electronic, mechanical, photocopying, recording or otherwise, without
the prior permission of NTC Publishing Group.
Manufactured in the United States of America.

  3 4 5 6 7 8 9 0 VP 9 8 7 6 5 4 3 2

ABOUT THE AUTHORS

Donald L. Ferguson and Jim Patten both have extensive experience in various journalism career fields.

Ferguson has experience in various media and related journalism positions. He has worked for newspapers, taught high school journalism and college journalism at The Ohio State University, The University of Nebraska and Baylor University. He provided public relations services for the Lincoln, Neb., school system and formed his own consulting firm, working with school districts and education associations throughout the United States. He managed a Denver-based public relations, advertising and opinion research firm. Ferguson has provided public relations services for Fortune 500 corporations and has been recognized for his expertise in crisis communications and investor relations by *Inside PR* magazine.

Patten is head of the Journalism Department at the University of Arizona in Tucson. During his journalistic career, he worked as reporter, editor, photographer, editorial writer, and columnist at nine newspapers. He previously taught at the University of Nebraska, Midland (Texas) College and the University of Texas at El Paso. Patten also serves as writing coach for professional journalists and is active in high school press issues. He is an award-winning teacher active in many professional journalistic groups.

Ferguson and Patten are co-authors of *Journalism Today!* and *The Journalism Today! Workbook,* published by NTC Publishing Group of Lincolnwood, Ill.

ACKNOWLEDGMENTS

For their assistance in preparation of this book, the authors wish to thank:

G. Donald Gale, Vice President,
>   News and Public Affairs, Bonneville
>   International Corporation, Salt Lake City, Utah

Leo Honeycutt

Thomas Pendleton

Stephen A. Smith

Todd Smith,
>   Bonneville, Washington, D.C., News Bureau

Arnold Smith, President,
>   The Smith Group, Washington, D.C.

The Dow Jones Newspaper Fund, Inc.

Our students, past, present, and future

FOREWORD

I do not know of a single soul who fell into this line of work. It is not the kind of job that you might want to do, it is work that you must do. There are, for some, enormous financial rewards, but generally the reward is in the work itself.

I wanted to be a reporter from the age of 16 and in the 42 years since then, I cannot recall a moment of genuinely wishing to be anything else. There are no special gifts required to succeed. An ability to write clear, concise sentences is important, as is a slavish devotion to precision. By that, I mean facts—not someone's interpretation of facts, but the genuine article. If you are too lazy or too sure of yourself to "go look it up," don't even think of becoming a reporter.

The most important gift is curiosity. You must have an insatiable hunger to know everything that is going on, from outer space to the locker room to behind the closed doors of the White House.

A reporter must have the ability to walk into perfect strangers' lives, ask the most personal kinds of questions, then leave without taking on their burdens. It does not mean that you become so hardened to human misery that you stop feeling. It simply means that you save those feelings for after hours, for your own time if you have any.

The work can be difficult and debilitating, and the company you may have to keep may not be the most companionable. But when you get your teeth into a good story, and all the pieces fall into place, and the facts are there—cold, hard, and shining—there is nothing, no job quite like this one. Good hunting to those of you who choose journalism as a career.

Morley Safer
CBS News

CONTENTS

Why choose journalism? The economic
rewards. Job satisfaction. Are you hooked yet?

Newspapers in Colonial America. Freedom of
the press. The development of modern
newspapers. The electronic media. Ethical
standards for journalists. Journalists'
functions.

Spelling—a sixth sense? A learnable skill.

CHAPTER 1

JOURNALISM:
A REWARDING CAREER

Columnist James Kilpatrick told this story many years ago in *Quill* magazine. A young man approached him for advice about becoming a newspaper reporter. Kilpatrick's visitor was 18, ready for college and wanted to select a career. Should it be journalism?

Kilpatrick's response was: "Don't be a newspaperman if you possibly can help it." The young man was startled. Today, of course, the young man interested in journalism is just as likely (possibly even more likely) to be a young woman, and the career question more likely to be about television. Kilpatrick's response, however, remains appropriate today.

Here's what he meant. Journalism is unlike any other craft. It most closely resembles show business. There's an undeniable element of ego in journalism, and an equally undeniable element of self-sacrifice. Performers know the show must go on. Journalists know the paper has to come out on time. They know the newscast has to be ready when the camera's red light goes on. If that means no day off this week, no coffee break tonight, no going home just because it's normal quitting time, those are the breaks. The work or "the public's interest" comes first.

WHY CHOOSE JOURNALISM?

Journalists talk about attraction to their work as a "calling," much the way ministers and surgeons do. Journalism is more than a job. It's a way of life. While sometimes it's exciting and exhilarating, it can be grindingly difficult and sometimes boring. Don't be a journalist unless you can't help it.

Most journalists can't help it. They talk of "getting hooked" in a high school journalism class or by taking a news job not knowing what they were getting into. They talk about the adrenalin rush that comes with covering a big story. They dismiss worries about deadline pressure. "That's when it's really fun," they say. "When there's a big story and you're matching wits against the deadline, that's great. It's not pressure. It's hard to believe somebody is actually paying us to do this."

Some recent studies, however, show that newspeople do pay a price. They seem to suffer more stress on the job than others. Many burn out before middle age and seek other careers. This worries some managers and the academics who do the studies. Yet journalism remains one of the most popular majors on most university campuses. Students see, and correctly so, the opportunity journalism provides for public service. Journalists affect the world.

So this book should carry a warning. Journalism can be addictive. Read on and face the possibility of getting hooked. If you don't *really* want the hard work of journalism, just say no now.

Some would-be journalists believe journalism is a glamorous life. There's a touch of truth to this. Some journalists uncover scandals that topple presidents and governors. Some cover Hollywood or Washington, D.C., and rub elbows with celebrities. Some write columns or become television anchorpeople and get rich and famous. But for every journalist in that category, at least fifty work in quiet anonymity.

Look at your daily paper. Sure it would be fun to be the reporter who wrote the lead story of the day, the one at the top of Page 1. But there's much more to the newspaper than that. Look lower on the front page. See the little weather box with tomorrow's forecast? A journalist wrote that, too. See the index items, directing readers to stories inside? A journalist wrote them. Turn to the sports page. See the long lists in small type of all the scores from yesterday's games? A journalist compiled them. Some papers run school lunch menus. A journalist does that. Check the Sunday paper. See all those "home of the week" stories in the real estate section. A journalist wrote those stories. Glamorous? Hardly.

One of the real keys to journalistic success and contentment is to love the *process* of journalism regardless of its content. That means enjoying news work whether you're writing a routine street–closing notice or the weather forecast or a two-paragraph account of a basketball game in an outlying town. The process matters, and those "little" stories require the same degree of accuracy, the same attention to detail that the big stories do. Journalism isn't for you if you have to be a superstar.

A small story will illustrate the point. In the newsroom one day, the city editor opened an envelope from a public relations firm. In the envelope was a press release, a proposed story offered to the newspaper by the public relations people of a local company. The press release was too long and had extraneous information. The city editor looked around. He spotted the newest, youngest member of the staff. He gave her the press release and asked her to rewrite it into news form. She blew up. "Why should I have to do something like that?" she asked. She saw the light when a senior journalist in the room, a man with thirty years in the business, took her aside and explained to her that even with all his experience he would be *happy* to rewrite the press release if asked. No one in the newsroom, he told her, can be above doing any job if that's what the paper needs at that moment.

THE ECONOMIC REWARDS

When one of the authors of this book, then 18 and much like the young man who approached Kilpatrick, told his high school journalism adviser that he had decided on a career in journalism, the adviser was pleased. "You won't make a lot of money but you'll sure have a lot of fun," he said. However, both parts of that statement are less true than they used to be.

At one time journalists almost had to take an oath of poverty. It was a price they paid for being journalists, for being in on the action and seeing the world close–up. Some beginning journalists have been known to make so little money that they qualified for food stamps! One college textbook, published as recently as the 1970s, actually said journalists can't make enough money to send their children to college.

This picture has changed. While it is true that salaries of journalists are still too low, they're rising fast. At the top levels of management, fears have been expressed that unless salaries go up, journalism will lose the best and the brightest of the next generation, and the nation will suffer as a result. A new emphasis on improving the financial lot of journalists is at work—and working. The recession of the early 1990s represents a setback for better journalistic salaries. Indeed, with a slipping economy, some journalists are out of work. Jobs for brand–new journalism graduates have dried up. Most people feel this is a temporary situation certain to improve when business (and therefore advertising) gets better.

Given the shelf life of a book, it's dangerous to use current figures. But it's important to get away from abstractions, too. These are approximate figures based on a variety of reports that take inflation into account. The starting salary for someone going into public relations just out of college is about $17,000 a year. A person starting in advertising can expect to make about $15,500. The new daily newspaper reporter will get about $14,500, and the new radio or television reporter about $13,500.

But these figures fall far short of telling the whole story. The beginning daily newspaper reporter lucky enough to land a job on an enlightened medium-sized daily (50,000 circulation or more) is likely to find his or her salary nearer $20,000. The same is true in public relations, advertising, and radio and television. There are plenty of exceptions to the figures in the previous paragraph. And of course the figures represent *beginning* salaries only. Most journalists with a few years on the job do much better. Five years down the road, the journalist who started at $14,500 is apt to be closer to $25,000, and later that figure can reach $40,000 or more. People in executive and management positions often make double or triple that. College tuition for your children shouldn't be a problem.

Besides, money is only one measure of job satisfaction. A study by the Dow Jones Newspaper Fund found 79 percent of recent graduates in mass media jobs to be either moderately or very satisfied with their jobs.

What would cause this satisfaction?

JOB SATISFACTION

We said earlier that the high school adviser's statement about having fun probably isn't as true as it once was. That's correct. Journalists (and here we're including advertising and public-relations people) are more responsible than they used to be. They're more concerned about ethics and truth, issues they struggle with daily. In the 1920s and the days of so–called Jazz Journalism, journalists considered their role almost exclusively a way to entertain themselves and their readers, in that order. If that meant fudging a bit with the facts or exaggerating a story, no problem. Today no such spirit prevails. Today the rules require accuracy and responsibility. And that means harder work for people in mass media jobs.

Still, the workers like their work. Why? Because journalism remains a craft where honesty and integrity are admired—and required. Sure journalists compromise sometimes. Nobody and no job is perfect. But the central ethic at this late date in the 20th Century remains: Serve the public with objective facts, honest advertising, open and candid public relations. The non-objective newspaper or newscast is soon rejected by the public. Not only is false advertising against the law, the fact is that it doesn't work. And the public–relations firm that hides company wrongdoing and publicizes only the "good things" soon finds it has lost its credibility.

In the ideal world of the classroom, all journalists are honest. No advertisers can call the publisher or station manager and kill a story by threatening to take away their advertising. No journalist ever takes sides in a story. No story ever gets killed because it offends the Chamber of Commerce. Yet all of these happen in the real world. They don't happen with anywhere near the frequency the public believes. No consistent pattern of subjective or biased reporting exists except in a tiny minority of standard newspaper or radio or TV news operations. (Here we discount the supermarket publications and their ELVIS IS ALIVE brand of "reporting.") No ten people in New York City dictate to all the nation's media what will be reported. The media are diverse (but becoming less so as more and more newspapers, for example, become parts of groups or chains).

Diversity is necessary. No thoughtful journalist will ever suggest one day's newspaper represents the total truth about what happened in the world the previous day. What that journalist will suggest, however, is that if the audience will read more than one newspaper, listen to radio newscasts, watch television newscasts (and not always the same station or network), and buy *Time, Newsweek,* or *U.S. News & World Report*, the truth will emerge.

ARE YOU HOOKED YET?

Surely, you must be thinking, in addition to all the other good things about journalism, the men and women who bring the nation its news and information are an admired species, attracting love and attention from an adoring audience. After all, information is essential in a democracy. Therefore, the bearers of this information must occupy a lofty position in society. Here we must disappoint you.

Journalists do *not* rate highly with the public. (In that regard, they are like some other institutions in the country: Congress and the Postal Service, for example.) Journalists often bring bad news. They report on wars and assassinations and corruption and fires and airplane crashes. Unable to do anything about the *message* in the media, some people get angry at the *media* themselves. Journalists can't react to this anger. Their job is to report the news. It's not their job to sugarcoat it. When the country went to war in the Persian Gulf and journalists screamed over what they saw as unnecessary censorship by the military, most Americans sided against the press. Journalists were not seen as particularly valuable people in that war, and the country was in no mood to join them in efforts to pry information from the government.

So don't expect to be popular. Polls confirm this. Close to 80 percent of the people in one recent U.S. poll said they believe the media unnecessarily invade people's privacy. One poll showed more than 80 percent think there should be a law *requiring* newspapers to report equally on both major candidates in the presidential race. The people believe this despite the fact that such a law would be unconstitutional. Of course newspapers *should* cover both candidates equally. But to *require* them to would violate the First Amendment to the Constitution, which guarantees freedom of the press (as well as other sacred liberties). And what would we do to editors whose newspapers didn't cover both candidates equally? Throw them in jail? Does that sound like the United States?

So, if you decide to take the plunge and go into a mass media job, don't expect to be popular. As someone put it, you'll be flogged by the public when you're right and you'll be flogged by the public when you're wrong. You'll be criticized from the political left and the political right.

But if you do the job right, if you follow the rules of accuracy and responsibility, if you serve the public and not yourself, you can have the inner satisfaction that comes with knowing your work is essential and that it serves, in the end, the cause of advancing our democracy and its people. That's the true reward of journalism.

CHAPTER 2

JOURNALISM THEN AND NOW

The journalist's job, it has been said, is to comfort the afflicted and afflict the comfortable. This oversimplified and overstated description of a complex craft contains a nugget of truth.

The statement suggests that conscientious journalists do their best to identify society's problems and to help solve them with clear, accurate information. By focusing on problems and issues, journalists provide information the public needs to find solutions. If homelessness is a problem, journalists zero in. Some may spend a few days and nights living on the streets and reporting what it's like. Thus informed, the hope is, the public will do something. This is the "comfort the afflicted" part.

As for "afflicting the comfortable," what journalists mean is they keep a constant eye on all forms of government. If the government is lax, corrupt, or dishonest, journalists report it so the public, mostly through the ballot box, will get better government. A fat cat public official, skimming public money for private use, has journalists to fear.

NEWSPAPERS IN COLONIAL AMERICA

It has always been that way in our country—even before there was a United States. In Colonial America, while we were still ruled by the British, journalists were busy comforting the afflicted and afflicting the comfortable. The American press was a partner to the American Revolution. The press exposed abuses by the British and fanned the flames of patriotism.

The Patriot papers weren't much like today's newspapers, of course. For one thing, they were openly partisan. If you wanted the other side, you had to buy a newspaper loyal to the other side. Today, ethical newspapers routinely print both sides of the news. The Patriot papers, on the other hand, planted the idea of revolution, and they encouraged rebellion.

The First Newspaper in America

Journalists in Colonial America were a particular target of the British Crown. That problem started with the very first newspaper in America. Printer Benjamin Harris published the newspaper and called it *Publick Occurrences Both Forreign and Domestick*. The newspaper appeared in 1690 in Boston. One story reported that ''a day of

Thanksgiving'' had been established by the Indians. But another story was critical of the king of France. That was enough for the government. It stepped in. *Publick Occurrences* was killed after only one edition. The official reason was that the newspaper had no license to print.

The idea of licensing a newspaper sounds strange to us today. Some members of the public do not understand this, but no one needs a license to print today. If you want to go to your home computer, create a newspaper and distribute it, you have every right to do so. You don't have to get anyone's permission, let alone buy a license. You are responsible for what you print, and if you libel someone, you may find yourself paying a great deal of money to that person. Still, you have the right to print.

In Colonial America, however, a license was required. The British Crown figured, and correctly so, that ideas were dangerous. So Harris's newspaper was killed.

The Boston Newsletter

Fourteen years passed before the Colonies again had a newspaper. The newspaper was John Campbell's *The Boston News-Letter,* and historians consider it the nation's first consecutively published newspaper. It first appeared in 1704 and had a monopoly in Boston for fifteen years. Underneath the newspaper's flag or nameplate (often incorrectly called its masthead), appeared the words, ''Published by Authority.'' This meant Campbell was licensed, and that the government approved his publication.

Campbell was loyal to the Crown so his newspaper was safe—as long as he remained loyal.

Anti-British Newspapers

Other newspapers began to appear. In 1721, the *New England Courant* appeared in Boston *without* the words "Published by Authority." The press had taken its first steps toward the great independence it enjoys today.

The Revolution was building steam. An event in 1735 stands out. John Peter Zenger ran *The New-York Weekly Journal*. It was a popular newspaper with the increasingly anti-British colonists. This made it *unpopular* with the British government, particularly Governor William Cosby. Cosby was a frequent target of the *Weekly Journal*. On November 17, 1734, Zenger was jailed, charged with seditious libel. In other words, he was charged with stirring up the people.

After months in jail, during which his wife Anna continued to print the paper, Zenger was brought to trial. In those days, all the government had to do was show that a seditious statement had been printed. It did not matter whether the criticism was true. In fact, the rule was "the greater the truth, the greater the libel." The government could easily turn aside a *false* criticism. It was the truth that hurt most. So if Zenger had printed what the government said he did, he would be guilty. At least that's what the government thought.

Zenger retained as his attorney Andrew Hamilton, considered by many the finest attorney in the Colonies even though he was then in his eighties. Hamilton readily conceded that Zenger had printed the stories the government said he had. To the government, the case had ended. But the government had underestimated Hamilton and Zenger—and the resistance in the Colonies to British rule. Hamilton told the court that if what Zenger printed was true then there could be no libel. For libel to occur, Hamilton argued, "the words themselves must be libelous—that is, false, malicious, and seditious—or else we are not guilty."

It took the jury only minutes to shout a verdict of "not guilty."

The trial not only gave a boost to the coming Revolution, but it helped establish a key legal principle still in effect today: Truth is a defense in libel. Libel must be false or it isn't libel.

By the time of the Revolution in 1775, thirty-seven newspapers were being printed in the Colonies. Most backed the Revolution.

FREEDOM OF THE PRESS

After the war, delegates to the Constitutional Convention in Philadelphia wrote the Constitution. When the framers of the Constitution, after meeting secretly, submitted it to the states for ratification, an outcry arose. The Constitution contained no reference to freedom of the press. Most state constitutions guaranteed that freedom. Nevertheless, in 1791, the Bill of Rights—the first ten amendments to the Constitution—was ratified. The First Amendment guaranteed freedom of the press.

American journalists enjoy a unique freedom. The First Amendment reads, "Congress shall make no law . . . abridging freedom of speech, or of the press." Frustrated government officials occasionally try to clamp down on the nation's free press, but the press almost always wins in such confrontations. The First Amendment is hard to defy.

THE DEVELOPMENT OF
MODERN NEWSPAPERS

After the war, and for the next two centuries, the nation grew rapidly, spreading from coast to coast. Hundreds of newspapers cropped up. Itinerant printers carried their clumsy typesetting equipment in wagons along with pioneers and settlers in the new lands. Even the smallest towns had newspapers, set by hand, one letter at a time. Soon the technology was to improve and with it the quality of newspapers.

Newspapers for the Working Class

In 1833, Benjamin Day founded the *New York Sun*. It was a revolutionary newspaper. Unlike its predecessors, the *Sun* was filled with news from the police beat and news about tragedies and natural disasters. It was written not for the intellectual elite but for the common person. And it sold for a penny.

The new working class created by the Industrial Revolution provided the *Sun* with a mass audience, which meant Day could attract more advertisers and charge them more for space in his paper. The formula is still in use today.

James Gordon Bennett founded the *New York Morning Herald* two years later. His paper cost two cents, but it copied Day's formula about news and advertising and it too succeeded. Then Horace Greeley followed suit, creating the *New York Tribune* in 1841 and attracting an unheard-of circulation of 200,000.

In 1841, Henry Raymond founded *The New York Times.* Today it is widely viewed as the best newspaper in the country and perhaps in the world. But it was not until Adolph Ochs bought it in 1896 that it became a distinguished newspaper. Today, its standards of fairness and accuracy are unsurpassed.

By 1910, after the Civil War and the invention of the telegraph, 2,600 daily newspapers were being published in the nation. Many cities had eight or ten newspapers. Today the country has about 1,700 daily newspapers and few but the largest cities have more than one.

Yellow Journalism

It could be said that this period, late in the nineteenth century and early in the twentieth, was journalism's adolescence. Journalism had not yet grown up. It was the era of "yellow journalism." The news was sensationalized and fabricated. Hoax stories made their way into print, surrounded by doctored photographs, bogus scoops, screaming headlines, and endless promotions of the newspapers themselves.

Some people insist to this day that newspapers whipped up enthusiasm for war that resulted in luring the United States into what became known as the Spanish-American War. William Randolph Hearst, publisher of the *New York Journal,* and Joseph Pulitzer, publisher of the *New York World,* were the most notable of the yellow journalists and are most often named by those suggesting the press led the nation into the Spanish-American war.

Muckraking

At this point newspapers got competition, and perhaps the competition led to the demise of yellow journalism. Magazines began to appear. *McClure's, Collier's,* and the *Saturday Evening Post* showed up on newsstands and demonstrated a new kind of journalism: muckraking. The muckrakers went after corruption, exposing big oil and patent medicine frauds and combatting child labor abuses. Many reforms resulted.

Jazz Journalism

Yellow journalism was followed by Jazz Journalism, another name for the same irresponsible brand of anything-goes "reporting." A racy and largely inaccurate picture of the world was painted daily by journalists more interested in their own amusement than in providing information to their audience.

THE ELECTRONIC MEDIA

Radio

Then came radio and more competition. The first radio newscast was in 1916 and regular programming began in 1920. The National Broadcasting Company (NBC) was formed in 1926, the Columbia Broadcasting System (CBS) in 1927. The Mutual Broadcasting System was launched in 1934 and renamed the American Broadcasting Company (ABC) in 1945.

Radio had a problem that the newspaper industry did not have. While one town could have ten newspapers—indeed, it could in theory have hundreds—the same was not true of radio. If radio broadcasts were not regulated, the airwaves would become a confused mass. Someone had to assign frequencies; someone had to keep the stations from bumping each other off the air. Since the airwaves are considered to be owned by society at large, the government stepped in. The Radio Act of 1927 was passed to keep the airwaves clear. The act created the Federal Radio Commission, forerunner to today's Federal Communications Commission, which regulates (not censors) both radio and television.

Today, Americans own something like 470 million radios. The stations number 4,700 on the AM band and 3,400 on FM. Radio's significance, however, pales in comparison to television, the most powerful communications instrument ever known.

Television

The first television newscast was in 1940. Most of the country first got television in the late 1940s and early 1950s. A national love affair with the tube began.

Today, a majority of Americans say they get most of their news from television. Most journalists, including most television journalists, are upset by this. While some television news shows are excellent, (''60 Minutes'' comes to mind), television news remains largely a headline service. A 30-minute newscast contains about as many words, not counting commercials, as there are in *one column* in a newspaper. Clearly, a citizen who relies exclusively on television for news will be under–informed. Some politicians know this, and run for public office on flimsy issues designed more to attract TV ''sound bites'' (often as short as ten seconds) than public debate on the real issues.

Today, American news and information media constitute a huge, high–tech industry bombarding us constantly with messages. These independent, constitutionally protected journalists play a pivotal role in society. While perhaps not as powerful as some people believe (the press cannot mold or manipulate your mind), the press certainly sets our national agenda. Journalists say, "We don't tell you what to think. But we do tell you what to think about." If it's on Page One of the paper and the lead story on the 11 P.M. news, it will be the talk of the town the next day.

ETHICAL STANDARDS FOR JOURNALISTS

What guides journalists? Certainly not the law. The printed media enjoy almost unlimited freedom to print whatever they see fit. The electronic media have only slightly less freedom—remember the public-owned air-waves—and with the demise of the FCC's Fairness Doctrine seem headed for equality with the printed media. No. The law doesn't guide them.

Journalists are guided by their ethical standards, often formalized into codes of ethics. Below are excerpts from various codes.

Code of the Society of Professional Journalists:

> The public's right to know of events of public importance and interest is the overriding mission of the mass media. The purpose of distributing news and

enlightened opinion is to serve the general welfare. Journalists who use their professional status as representatives of the public for selfish or other unworthy motives violate a high trust.

Freedom of the press is to be guarded as an inalienable right of people in a free society. It carries with it the freedom and the responsibility to discuss, question, and challenge actions and utterances of our government and our public and private institutions. Journalists uphold the right to speak unpopular opinions and the privilege to agree with the majority.

Journalists at all times will show respect for the dignity, privacy, rights and well-being of people encountered in the course of gathering and presenting the news.

Radio-Television News Directors Association Code of Broadcast News Ethics:

The primary purpose of broadcast journalists—to inform the public about events of importance and appropriate interest in a manner that is accurate and comprehensive—shall override all other purposes.

Broadcast news presentations shall be designed not only to offer timely and accurate information, but also to present it in the light of relevant circumstances that give it meaning and perspective. This standard means that news reports, when clarity demands it, will be laid against pertinent factual background; that factors such as race, creed, nationality or prior status will be reported only when they are relevant; that comment or subjective content will be properly identified and that errors in fact will be promptly acknowledged and corrected.

Code of Professional Standards of the Public Relations Society of America:

> A member shall deal fairly with clients or employers, past, present, or potential, with fellow practitioners, and with the general public.
>
> A member shall adhere to truth and accuracy and to generally accepted standards of good taste.
>
> A member shall not intentionally communicate false or misleading information, and is obligated to use care to avoid communication of false or misleading information.

Unlike the codes that guide doctors or lawyers, journalists' codes have no teeth. An unethical lawyer can be disbarred. An unethical doctor can lose his/her license. An unethical journalist can (and will) be fired. But he or she can't be penalized by the state for ethical misconduct. Nor can he or she lose a license. It would be unconstitutional for a journalist to have to have a license.

JOURNALISTS' FUNCTIONS

We expect journalists to provide clear, accurate, unbiased information. For the most part, they do just that, often against great odds (hostile sources, uncaring audiences). How can we judge how well they do? Journalists have roles assigned them, informally, in our society. By knowing these roles and monitoring their work, it's possible for an informed citizen to determine how well they're fulfilling their roles.

The Political Function

Perhaps the most important job assigned to the press is to monitor the activities of government. This is called the political function. The press calls it its watchdog role. The First Amendment is in place to guarantee that the press is able to perform this function. A press fearful of government would not make much of a watchdog. Freedom of the press is there so our system of checks and balances will work. The press has no higher duty.

The Entertainment Function

Life is not all City Council meetings and politics. We also expect the press to entertain us. That's why Dear Abby and the comic strips are there. The political function is far more important to society than the entertainment function but most journalists concede that government news often can be dull. So if your morning paper or evening newscast makes you smile, that's the entertainment function at work.

The Social Function

The press has a social function, too. What we talk about, what we think about during a day are apt to have come to us from the media. The old small-town America of backyard, barber-shop, and around-the-crackerbarrel conversation is long gone. Now, yesterday's headlines are today's conversations.

The Economic Function

The press also has an economic function, fulfilled through advertising and news of business products. The nation's economy needs healthy mass media to keep the economic wheels turning.

The Record-keeping Function

And the press keeps the record for us. Who is born, who dies, who gets married, who gets divorced, what the president said yesterday, who won the big game, and so on. The record-keeping function, though hardly glamorous or dramatic, is an important one.

CHAPTER 3

WRITING: THE KEY TO ALL
JOURNALISM CAREERS

Walk into any journalism classroom on the first day of the semester and you'll hear the teacher saying something about like this:

> Journalists are hard-working and tenacious. They don't take no for an answer. They don't quit until the job is finished. They're curious. They're creative. They enjoy people and care about them. They're well-informed on current events.

The list could go on. What the teacher is trying to do is identify the characteristics of journalists. This probably is a waste of time.

Journalists are like everybody else. They come in all varieties. Many are outgoing. But you can be shy and be a journalist. Many are assertive. But you can be low–key and be a journalist. Many are tough. But you can be a softie and be a journalist. No one should reject journalism as a career because he or she doesn't fit some old movie's stereotype of what journalists are like. The best advice still is "be yourself."

But successful journalists do share one trait. All of them can write. It is the fundamental skill, whether you want to go into newspapers or magazines, print or broadcast, public relations or advertising. Someone writes every broadcast, every story, headline or caption, every news release, every advertisement. The ability to craft clear, powerful sentences is required of all journalists, no matter what part of the business they're in. So don't spend your time in English class daydreaming about conquering the world of journalism. You'll need the writing skills your English teacher is showing you.

Some journalists are virtual geniuses with the language. Most are not. Most are skilled craftspeople who have trained their eyes and ears to recognize bad writing and to punch the delete key. (We used to say good writers have big wastebaskets. Now we say good writers wear out the delete key. Zap the bad sentences.)

Some journalists struggle with writing, of course. The business is full of stories about great reporters who couldn't write a word. Some of those stories are true. But every year sees fewer and fewer poor writers succeeding in journalism. Jobs are scarce. The people doing the hiring can be choosy.

"So where does that leave me?" we can imagine many readers asking. "I get C's in my English classes, spend three times as long on essays and term papers as my classmates and still get my papers back covered with red ink. And spelling? It's beyond me. English is a hard language.''

SPELLING—A SIXTH SENSE?

This statement raises many issues. Let's take spelling first. Some people are blessed with almost a sixth sense about spelling. They're able to spell a word correctly the first time they hear it. This ability appears to be genetic. Others are less fortunate. They can do math but not words. They're great mechanics but don't ask them how to spell "accommodate." They can't do it. And our spelling whiz probably can't change a tire.

Learning theorists, however, reject this thinking. Everyone can learn how to change a tire. And everyone can learn to spell. Many people simply memorize the words, a few at a time, the way spelling used to be taught in the lower grades. Others undertake formal study of the rules of English. "I before E except after C" is still a good rule to know. And there are many others, of course. (Is it "cemet*a*ry" or "cemet*e*ry?" Remember that everyone in the cemetery is at ease, and think of "ease" as E's. It's all E's. Cem*e*t*e*ry.) The best thing someone with spelling problems can do, however, is wear out two dictionaries a year looking up words. It's no crime to be a poor speller. It *is* a crime not to get the dictionary habit and look up the words. If you're working on a computer, get a spell-checking program, and run it on everything you write. The spelling problem can be solved.

A LEARNABLE SKILL

What about the other problems facing our imaginary writer? All those C's in English and all those hours working on essays only to have them covered with red ink? Talent plays a role here, of course. Just as some people have good spelling genes, so do some have good writing genes. In the movie "Amadeus," Wolfgang Amadeus Mozart had talent, and the music he wrote came effortlessly. His hapless rival, Antonio Salieri, had to work harder and the music wasn't as good. *But it wasn't bad, either.* And today the record and compact disk stores sell Salieri's works as well as Mozart's.

Hard work and perseverance can go a long way toward overcoming lack of natural talent. The words may not flow for you the way they do for the Mozart at the next desk. But that doesn't make everyone else's words unimportant. Just harder. Yes, English is a hard language. Hard. Not impossible.

One way to improve your writing ability is by reading, and not just newspapers or magazines either. Read the back of the cereal box at breakfast. Read the signs on the bus on the way to school. Always have a novel going. Carry it with you and read a paragraph whenever you have a spare moment. Haunt the library. Read books *about* writing. And read and memorize what all those remarks in red ink are about!

No one denies that writing is hard work. To be sure, there are days when the words flow and your fingers dance over the keys magically. Such days are to be treasured because for most of us they come rarely.

The Writing Process

Most people would rather do anything than get started writing. Watch them sometime. A typical journalism student comes back to the newsroom or classroom after a reporting assignment and a ritual begins. First something to drink. Then a chat with a friend. Then maybe the computer keys need brushing off. Or the screen cleaned. Finally, it's time to write. And nothing comes out. Somebody once said writing is easy, ''You just stare at the screen until blood appears on your forehead.''

When it's time to write, the thing to do is write. Get started. You'll probably throw out the first three or four paragraphs you write while your mind's warming up. That's fine. Hit the delete key. Once you're under way, it almost always gets easier. And when you're done, the rewards are great. The author of ''The Seven C's of Writing'' offers the following reassurances:

> At the end you never know that what you've done is the best you can do. Nor do you know for certain that the reader is going to read what you've written. But there's a thrill that comes from seeing your

handiwork in print that more than compensates for the turmoil and the struggle. Then it dawns on you that by golly you've done *something*. By having the strength, tenacity, and courage to display your abilities and your convictions, you've reached, affected, and motivated hundreds, perhaps thousands, of your fellow human beings. ("The Seven C's of Writing)

Writing is, at least in part, a collection of tricks. Perhaps things like rhythm and color and beauty are difficult to attain except for literary Mozarts. Yet, some of what constitutes good writing is simple and learnable. Anyone can master tight writing.

Tight Writing

Every editing book contains long lists like this short one intended to introduce the notion of editing for tightness. Don't write bouquet of flowers. Just write bouquet. Don't write made arrangements. Write arranged. Don't write made a decision. Write decided. Don't write Easter Sunday. Easter is always on Sunday. Don't write Jewish rabbi. All rabbis are Jewish. Don't write due to the fact that. Write because. Don't write new recruit. All recruits are new. Just write recruits. Can you detect the wordiness in "present incumbent," "rough estimate," "basic fundamentals"? Of course. It's a trick. Anyone can learn it.

Grammar and Usage

The rules of grammar and usage are written down and learnable. Nouns and pronouns have to agree. Subjects and verbs have to agree. Some of it is tricky. Most of it is not. If you're interested in journalism, you must be interested in language. This is fundamental and will not change no matter what new technology appears. Computers don't write; people do.

Many journalists are word freaks who get great joy out of unusual words or word combinations. Many headline writers are punsters. Many a game of Scrabble has been played around newsroom copydesks late at night after the newspaper is finished. If you want into journalism, get into words.

Care and precision in language are not out of your reach. Remember that "farther" and "further" are different words with different meanings. Note that "anxious" and "eager" are not interchangeable. Do not call the man being married the groom. A groom cares for horses. The man at the altar is the bridegroom.

Even people with bad writing genes can learn the difference between "affect" and "effect," "principle" and "principal," "libel" and "liable," "guerrilla" and "gorilla," "capital" and "capitol." Your spell-checking program will sail right past those words because they're spelled all right (there is no such word as "alright"). So you'll have to know the difference.

Knowing the words on this small list is not a huge accomplishment. Filling your head with dozens and dozens of these types of distinctions, however, is a big step on the road to good writing. And you don't have to be Mozart to be able to do it.

No one has ever been forced to use a cliche. No one *has* to use jargon or fuzzy language. No one is compelled to write long, unwieldy sentences. Euphemisms can be avoided. All of these enemies of good writing can be recognized and axed. No mystery here. Just common sense.

In an essay, Clarke Stallworth of the *Birmingham (Ala.) News* once made this common-sense observation:

> Good writing is clear. Bad writing is not.
>
> That's the big difference between the two. Why is the difference so important?
>
> To begin with, clear writing holds the reader. The reader's eye moves along the line of familiar, friendly words, cruising smoothly across the page. No breaks, no potholes, and the reader concentrates on the message. And the golden spark of communication arcs between writer and reader.
>
> If the writing is clear, the writer can use a whole arsenal of good writing techniques—he or she can make pictures, tell stories, use lively verbs, slice out jargon and unnecessary words and cliches, put people in the story, show rather than tell.

Later he added this guideline:

> Put the 10-20-30 yardstick on the writing. If your average paragraph is 30 words or less, you're probably OK. If your average sentence is 20 or below, you're

probably in the ball game. And if your percentage of big words is less than 10 percent (5 percent is better), then you're in the writing business.

The principles are easy to state and easy to follow. Use short words, short sentences, short paragraphs. Spell the words right. Follow the rules of grammar. Avoid cliches, jargon, fancy words, euphemisms. Edit carefully; few written efforts are perfect on the first try. Read widely. Try to write every day.

Benjamin Bradlee, executive editor of the *Washington Post,* was talking about reporters when he said the following. His words apply as well to everyone considering a career in journalism:

> The best reporters are those who combine energy, judgment, curiosity, fairness, skepticism, commitment and knowledge with the ability to express themselves with grace and clarity.

CHAPTER 4

THE NATURE OF NEWSPAPER WORK

The word "variety" springs to mind in describing the work of newspaper journalists. So much goes into creating a newspaper that people with all types of talents can find a place there. Reporters, writers, headline writers, artists, page designers, editors, and specialists of many kinds are needed.

Further, newspapers vary so much in how often they come out, what audiences they serve, what their circulations are that there's no correct way to lump them under the one term "newspaper." Newspapers offer a variety of jobs in a variety of circumstances.

The usual, generic concept of "newspaper" is that of a daily product that tries to cover, first, a city, then a state, then the nation, then the world. The United States has about 1,700 daily newspapers that generally do just that.

But they vary too. Some have many editions a day and a blockbuster edition on Sunday. Some papers come out five times a week plus Sunday, usually skipping the Saturday edition. Some publish five times a week and take the weekend off. And more than 5,000 newspapers come out on a non-daily basis, that is, once, twice or even three times a week.

Some newspapers, no matter how often they come out, ignore the general news completely, aiming their information at specialized audiences. These audiences might be senior citizens or members of a religious group. They might be campers, exercise enthusiasts or collectors. "Newspaper" is a rich term.

That aside, in some respects newspapers are all alike. At least the processes they use are alike. Someone assigns the stories to be gathered, reporters gather and write the stories, editors check them for various things, someone decides on pictures or artwork, someone does a layout, someone writes the headlines and captions. This is as true at the weekly *Dawson County Herald* in Lexington, Neb., as it is at the huge metropolitan daily *Philadelphia Inquirer.* The processes vary little.

Someone even said all newspapers *smell* alike, a not unpleasant mixture of ink, paper, photographic chemicals—and sweat.

REPORTERS

In examining what people at newspapers do, reporters come first because they're the eyes and ears of the newspaper and the people it serves. No newspaper is any better than its reporting staff. Great photographs, great headlines, great layouts . . . all amount to little if the reporting isn't there. Looking at it another way, if the reporting *is* there, the photographs, headlines, and layouts are still secondary. Important, yes, but less important than the information found by reporters.

At a weekly newspaper, reporters often also are photographers, illustrating their own stories. Then they may switch hats and edit the copy, write the headlines and do the layout. They may even find themselves helping with production, pasting up pages and placing artwork on the pages. At the *smallest* papers, the reporter might even help distribute the paper or sell paperclips at the counter.

Many ranking newspaper editors prefer reporters who began their careers at small papers, not necessarily nondaily papers, but at papers where everybody does everything. It's dangerous to specialize too early. Some time on the police beat, some time covering education, sports or the courts can be valuable in providing the groundwork for general reporting. Reporters who start at a larger paper may never come to understand the entire process, but instead learn only about their small corner of the newsroom. Reporters at a small paper absorb even the economics of newspaper publishing. Most reporters probably prefer to remain aloof from newspaper economics, but that's a luxury. In these bottom-line days, everyone needs to know about money.

Many types of reporters ply their trade at newspapers. Many are specialists, covering business or the judicial system. Some specialize in international coverage or minority affairs or religion. Such reporters generally are free of the responsibility of covering breaking news: the airplane crash, the fire, the surprise news conference. Most set their own assignments. In an ideal situation, they tell the editors what they're working on rather than the other way around.

General Assignment Reporters

General assignment reporters (GA's) come to work every day not knowing for sure what they're going to be doing. They're sent where needed. One day they might attend an announcement of this week's lottery winners. The next day they might find themselves doing a story about the construction causing traffic jams downtown. And the following day, they might interview the winner of the local spelling bee. They're generalists, and they have to be able to produce good copy rapidly.

Beat Reporters

Beat reporters cover the same agencies or subject-matter areas all the time. Typical beats are police, schools or education, courthouse, business, statehouse, the Legislature, the governor's office, science and medicine. Beat reporters deal with the same sources day after day and must develop relationships with them. They have to demonstrate a track record of accuracy and fairness to their sources or they can be cut off. If they develop that record, then sources will open up to them, provide tips, and offer copies of reports and documents. Beat reporters whose sources don't trust them can't be effective. Winning this trust requires considerable people skill.

One danger if reporters stay on the same beat too long, is they can begin to *think* like their sources. Or write like them. There's nothing worse than an education writer whose stories start sounding like interoffice memos at the local university. It's possible for beat reporters to get too close to their sources, to develop friendships that can interfere with news judgment when a source/friend becomes the object of criticism, for example.

Some Washington, D.C., reporters, it is said, have been known to start *dressing* like the U.S. senators they cover—dark suits, power ties, the little half glasses like those Senator Edward Kennedy wears. Many newspapers rotate beat reporters off their beats every once in awhile to avoid these problems.

Beat reporters, incidentally, also usually make their own assignments; they know better about what's happening on their beats than their editors do.

Lifestyle Reporters

Lifestyle or feature reporters are a blend of many talents. Rather than working out of the city desk on hard–news material, they specialize in trend stories, consumer, stories, food stories, book and restaurant reviews, and the whole array of material newspapers present that doesn't fit as hard news.

Such writers are usually free to explore different writing styles, to "featurize" their work more. And they live on off–beat ideas. Hard–news journalists sometimes look down on the feature section, asking feature writers as they walk past the city desk, "Hey, you working on a late-breaking recipe today?" Feature writers' work is much approved by the audience, however. And there is no question that today's newspapers, for better or worse, are placing more emphasis on feature stories than they did in the past. As newspaper circulation declines, editors search for a formula that will help them win back readers—and they often look to the soft news.

Investigative Reporters

A few larger newspapers have investigative reporters or investigative teams. They work on longer projects, sometimes spending as much as a year on one story or series of related stories. Often they work in secret, with only senior editors aware of their projects. They tend to write exposes and to uncover wrongdoing or corruption. They also became investigative reporters after long years as general assignment or beat reporters.

Investigative reporters spend a great deal of time poring over records in musty courthouses, chasing down telephone records, filing Freedom of Information Act requests with the government to pry loose information the government would rather not give out. Being an investigative reporter can be tedious work. But it pays off in benefits to society when a wrong is righted—and it pays off in prizes that can enhance a newspaper's reputation.

Sports Reporters

Sports reporters do much the same thing as their counterparts in features or on beats. Most newspapers divide the various athletic endeavors of their town or region and assign a reporter to each. Someone covers the university's teams, several handle local high schools, and senior reporters cover the professional teams. Beginning sportswriters tend to cover high schools—or even bowling or outdoor sports.

Interestingly, it can be harder to cover high schools than major college or professional sports. Sportswriters covering high school have to keep their own statistics and cover the games as well. At a pro or big-college game, the writers can concentrate on the game. Representatives of the teams or schools bring the statistics—not to mention coffee—in the pressbox and even bring photocopied quotes from coaches and players if the writers don't have time for post–game interviews.

Sportswriting poses the same dangers beat reporting does: Sportswriters can get too close to their teams. They can become cheerleaders, advocates of the team instead of advocates of good information *about* the teams.

Some of the best writers on most newspapers are in the sports department, often unfairly called the toy shop by the hard–nosed, hard–news citizens at the city desk.

A large amount of every reporter's time is spent on the telephone. A reporter trying to do two stories at once has to work the telephone—quite a skill in itself—and stay close to it. Run out to a source's office, and you might miss three important calls while you're away. Reporters use many techniques, but mostly they call and call, ask and ask, verify and verify. They read documents, attend meetings, attend news briefings—and always they wait for sources to return calls. Perseverance and patience are good qualities for any reporter.

COPY EDITORS

Reporters and copy editors make up the two largest groups of people at most newspapers. They complement each other even if they don't always compliment each other.

They need to work together although tensions often arise between them. Reporters don't like seeing their copy changed. Copy editors have their own opinions about how stories should be presented. *Wise* reporters know how often good copy editors save them embarrassment or inaccuracies, however, and treasure the good editors.

A description of a copy editor's work will make it sound almost clerical or routine. It's anything but. Copy editors are essential to the production of good newspapers.

After a reporter writes a story, a city editor or an assistant city editor looks at it, depending on the size of the newspaper. Then the story goes to the copy desk. At smaller newspapers, there may be no one between the reporter and the copy desk. At the copy desk, the head of the desk will glance at the story and assign it to a copy editor.

Copy editors do many things with the story. They check it for spelling, grammar, and punctuation. They check it for style, that is, they see that it conforms with the newspaper's stylebook. (The stylebook is a set of rules requiring that certain words or concepts be expressed the same way by everyone on the staff. A newspaper can't write ''adviser'' in one paragraph and ''advisor'' in the next, even though both are correct spellings. The stylebook dictates which to use.) Copy editors check a story for organization: Is the lead (the most important news) in the seventh paragraph? If so, the copy editor may ask the story's reporter to rewrite it. (Here's where the tension can come in.) If that's not possible, the copy editor may rewrite it, or kick it back to the city desk for the revision.

Copy editors watch for libel, poor taste, inaccuracies, unclear sentences, misspelled names of people or streets or buildings, wordiness, cliches, and jargon.

If a copy editor misses something, it almost certainly will get in the paper. Production staffers who used to catch the errors of journalists in the back shop have largely been eliminated by the technology. So there is no backup for the journalists. That's why this work definitely isn't clerical.

When copy editors finish editing a story, they then have to perform a crucial task. Copy editors write the headlines. (On a small paper, of course, reporters might write their own heads. But on a paper of any size at all, copy editors do this.) Headline writing is a job that requires speed, great word skills, imagination, and precision.

Copy editors have to condense the main points of a story, in an attractive and eye-catching way, into as few as three or four or five words. It's not easy. Good headline writers are worth their weight in gold in any newsroom.

Like reporters and all newspaper employees, copy editors do their work at computer terminals. The days of pencil and paper and messy glue are, thankfully, gone. Computer technology has placed new pressure on the copy desk. Some tasks once done in the composing room by printers are now done at the copy desk.

Thus, the best place for a new journalism school graduate looking for work is on the copy desk. That's where the jobs are. Make sure it's for you, however. Copy desk work requires people with top-notch language skills and an eye for detail. The hours tend to be more regular than those reporters work. They may be *odd* hours, though. Some copy editors start work at 2 A.M. Others come in at 6 A.M. Some start at 5:30 in the afternoon. Generally, though, they work eight hours and go home—even if they're driving home at 3 A.M.

LAYOUT AND PAGE DESIGNERS

Layout and page design staffers are the newspaper's visual people. They design the pages to make them attractive and easy to read. Working on their own or under the direction of an editor, they decide where on a page to place the various elements—photos, artwork, charts or graphs, and stories.

This isn't just mechanical work. It's journalism. What message are we sending our readers by putting this story at the top of the page and this one at the bottom? What balance can we achieve, both graphically and journalistically, by mixing state and local news, by placing related stories together?

Techniques in newspaper design are improving, and so is the technology these journalists use. Pushed by *USA Today,* most newspapers are putting new emphasis on color, and this challenges page designers to use it creatively. Staff artists usually work closely with the page-design staff, creating graphics, charts, and maps, under deadline, on their own computers.

EDITORS

Depending on the size of the paper, one editor may run the whole show. Or there may be twenty people with "editor" as part of their title. Editors are bosses. They set policy. Some set policy and stand back and watch. Others set policy and then roll up their sleeves and help carry it out (a practice that doesn't always please the staff).

At most newspapers, the top-ranking journalist is known as the managing editor, although executive editor is a fairly common title, too. The m.e. decides what the paper is going to be about, sitting in on news meetings, suggesting some stories and vetoing others. He or she (usually he, frankly, but we're working on it), does most of the hiring and firing and generally sets the tone for the paper.

The m.e. may have several a.m.e.'s (assistant managing editors) or he or she may have none. The assistant managing editors usually have a specific territory to watch over, a.m.e for graphics, a.m.e for features, for example.

The city editor directs the local reporting staff. He or she has to juggle dozens of stories, answer staff questions constantly, make instant news decisions, and help guide the overall philosophy of the paper. The city editor is like a general in a battle. Where should we send our forces? How big is this story and can we get a reporter there in time to cover it? The city editor sits on a hot seat between reporters and higher-ranking editors and sometimes feels great pressure from both. Many reporters aspire to be city editor; it's a prestigious job. But it's a hard one that doesn't permit much relaxing at work.

Most papers have a news editor. when all the m.e.'s and a.m.e.'s are gone, the news editor gets the paper out, making news, coverage and layout decisions by the minute. This person is on the spot and must be able to react quickly to changing news situations.

If ranking editors decide in a meeting at 5 P.M. what will be in the paper the next day, the news editor will be there at 11 P.M. when a plane crashes—and has to be able to fit the new situation with the 5 P.M. decisions. If you like to be in charge, if you like deadline pressure . . . this is the best job at any newspaper.

COLUMNISTS

A lucky few people get to write their own columns, to express their opinions under their bylines every day or every week. Some people consider this a premium job. Others cringe at the idea of having to produce a signed, inventive, readable, thoughtful piece on a regular basis. They consider it a real chore.

Columnists, no matter how many columns they may be ahead, talk about how they're always nagged by the next column they must produce. You see them wandering around the newsroom, reading, talking—anything to get an idea.

Some of the best–read items in any newspaper are columns. Some of the best–paid people in any newspaper are columnists. They have tremendous influence in some cities, and some personalities—like Mike Royko of the *Chicago Tribune*—become nationally famous.

Journalistic beginners would be advised, however, to get an education, learn the basics and make their way up the ladder before turning to columns. There's a long line ahead of you.

EDITORIAL CARTOONISTS

Another long line. Editorial cartoonists are a special breed of people. They have to be artists, and they have to be journalists and critics. An editorial cartoonist who is merely a good artist but who has nothing to say won't go far. Nor will someone who is a great social critic but can't draw.

College newspapers are a great place to cut your teeth if editorial cartooning is what you'd like to do. Most college newspapers would like good, locally produced cartoons. Most have no such thing.

If this is your interest, prepare five or six cartoons on local subjects and go see the editor. As for a course of study, get your academic adviser to explore a combination of art, political science, and journalism.

EDITORIAL WRITERS

Editorial writers are like columnists in a way. They have to produce all the time, on the creative days as well as the dry ones. The one difference is that editorial writers usually are anonymous. What they write represents the paper's viewpoint, not necessarily their own. Which can be a problem. Sometimes editorial writers believe one thing and have to write another, although larger newspaper have staffs big enough that this usually can be avoided.

Most editorial writers were once reporters or editors who opted for editorial writing because they have something to say and the skills to say it well. They need to be good researchers and, yes, good reporters. Some editorial writers just read stories, look at the ceiling, and then comment. The best ones, however, do their reporting by making phone calls and checking old files and generally getting first-hand information before offering opinions.

PHOTOGRAPHERS

Like page designers, photographers are visual people. Photography is more than setting the camera, focusing, and shooting. It has its technical side, of course, but the best photographers are artists, with keen visual instincts combined with the instincts of the best reporters, who somehow always come back with the story. Good photographers always come back with the picture. Some of their work is closely directed by editors. A good deal of it, however, is of their own choosing.

Photographers also have to be darkroom technicians at most papers—and some are reporters, too, at smaller papers. *All* photographers should be part reporter. There's nothing as discouraging (or typical) as a conversation between an editor and a photographer in which the editor wants the *names* of the people in the picture—and the photographer doesn't have them!

CHAPTER 5

CAREERS IN ELECTRONIC MEDIA

In addition to offering music, entertainment, and advertising, radio and television offer the journalist excellent career alternatives in broadcast news.

Over a half-billion radios are in operation today in the United States and Canada, receiving signals from over 10,000 AM and FM radio stations. Nearly all households in America have at least one television set. More than 2,000 television stations send us news and information. Hundreds of special interest media also exist to serve special audiences—educational, religious, minorities. In addition, nearly 7,000 cable television systems offer a variety of local, news, and special–interest channels throughout the nation.

More and more Americans, perhaps a majority, rely on electronic media for daily news, sports, and information about the events and issues shaping their lives. The electronic media, through increasingly effective technology, bring today's news and events to us as they happen, anywhere in the world.

REQUIREMENTS FOR A
BROADCASTING CAREER

Writing Skill

The most critical skill in handling radio and television news is the same as in other journalism careers—writing. Learning the basic skills for newswriting will prepare you for adapting those skills to the special needs of the broadcast media. Read the lead story in today's newspaper. Then watch that story on television. The newspaper is not constrained by time. The stories are longer, offer more insights and depth, go behind the scenes to provide detailed reports by observers, and provide background information important to understanding the implications of the story. Broadcast media, however, have only a few minutes—sometimes seconds—to tell the story, unless the broadcast is a news special. Aided by visual material, you see the event as it is described by the reporter on the scene or in the television newsroom. On the radio you hear an even more brief report of the event, often including comments from participants.

Clarity in broadcast copy becomes even more critical. The key at that point—and something that could determine your success as a broadcast journalist—is what *not* to include in the story. Television newscasts seldom contain more than 15 minutes of news, yet it is arguably where most busy people get their news. In those 15 minutes, newscasters have to tell you everything that happened around the world and around your town. What's more, as broadcast journalists move from one market to a larger one, they are required to tell more and more in less and less time. Even videotaped stories that reporters have worked on all day or perhaps days, as a rule of thumb, seldom receive more than 90 seconds of air time within a newscast.

That's why clarity in writing is critical from the start. Short, descriptive, well–constructed sentences are the rule. Not only can the listener follow the story more clearly, the announcer can say the words more clearly.

But the journalists' job in all three media—newspaper, radio and television—is the same—to report the story accurately, fairly, and as completely as possible within the format and time limitations of the specific medium. You work equally hard to uncover the news story for your audience.

Experience

Not unlike applying for most jobs, your personal presentation, appearance, and personality will play a dominant role in getting hired. Next to writing skills, experience is critical. Internships will place you ahead of those without such experience. A study for the U.S. Radio-Television News Directors Association (RTNDA) by The Roper Organization Inc. indicated that three-fourths of the radio and television stations offer internships. That same survey also showed that more than half of those internships were unpaid.

You may want to find part-time jobs at local broadcast media while in high school and throughout college. Don't overlook the student radio and television stations and educational broadcast media as laboratories for real world experience. These jobs don't necessarily have to be in the news department. Any media job helps you learn how the business functions, what reporters do, and gives you a clearer understanding of the craft. You also get your foot in the door so that you can be considered for other jobs as they become available.

Education

In the RTNDA study, more than 70 percent of the electronic media surveyed indicated that a four-year undergraduate education is either absolutely essential or important to a broadcast career. News directors surveyed strongly (70 percent) rate a journalism/communications degree important in evaluating candidates for jobs. About 20 percent ranked graduate degrees as important to a broadcast career.

Survey respondents said among the jobs available for graduating college students in broadcasting, 32 percent were in the newsrooms.

Don't be unrealistic about the first job in broadcast journalism. Beginning salaries are not high, starting often at $14,000–$15,000, depending on the size of the market and station. Advancement may be slow and turnover in the top jobs infrequent, especially in television.

RADIO CAREERS

Tape recorders, car phones, radios. Modern technology helps the radio journalist bring you the sounds of events as they happen or record them for use on regular newscasts. Live reports from a fire or hazardous waste spill; reports from a news conference or the locker room after a major sports event; and interviews with people making today's news all come from the radio journalist.

The number of jobs in radio news will depend on the size of the station and the community it serves. Many small stations may have only a few journalists to compile today's news from extensive wire services and audio news networks providing summaries of events from around the world and on special topics, such as business, agriculture, the weather, entertainment, and sports. Larger stations may have specialists who report news in these and other areas. Stations that specialize in providing all news all day will draw from many sources—staff, radio broadcast services, and wire services.

News Director

The news director organizes and plans the day's coverage. If the station has news reporters, they're assigned by the director to cover events of the day and to prepare other special news reports. In smaller stations, the news director often will write and edit the news as well as deliver the newscast.

Larger radio stations will have editors who compile the news from the wires and audio news networks. Individuals specializing in sports, farm news, business news, entertainment news, or other specialized topics will prepare information for the newscaster to deliver on–air or prepare taped or live reports themselves for use in newscasts or at specific broadcast times.

JOBS IN TELEVISION NEWS

Similarly, television newsrooms are served by a variety of wire services and video networks. We have all become familiar with the leading U.S and Canadian national television networks—ABC, CBS, NBC, CBC, CTV and Fox network. But we also have seen an increase in recent years in the variety and length of local news coverage in many communities. Local stations hire staff in the capitol to ''feed'' (report, videotape a presentation, and send it by satellite to the local station) the story for use in tonight's news. Trucks are equipped with satellite transmission capabilities that, when linked with camera equipment virtually anywhere, can bring live reports from the scene of an airline crash that may have occurred only minutes ago; the site of a shuttle launch; or a state parade or a post-game celebration. We see police invade crack houses and share the emotion of a presidential inauguration. Technology makes it possible for us to be a part of today's news as it happens, or to see it as it happened within only a few minutes.

News Director

Television jobs are increasing in number in many communities where there is a growing emphasis on news. The TV news director is responsible for managing the news operations. Staff is hired and fired, reporters assigned to stories, editors directed in preparation of video stories, camera operation organized, and news and sportscasts scripted under the eye of the news director. News directors usually have worked their way through the ranks, serving several years as reporters, editors, or newscasters. Some come through newspaper careers or after years in radio news. They are ultimately responsible for what we see and hear on television news programs.

Larger stations may have managing editors to assist the news director. A managing editor supervises the daily operations, while executing the plans outlined by the news director.

Producers and Directors

Producers and directors (sometimes one person has both titles) put the news show together. These people bring the video from the scene of the news together with the news-caster; they also make sure that slides, charts, graphs, or other visual material are ready and in the proper order. They are responsible for the product we actually see and hear during the allocated time period. Larger stations will have assistants in these areas who may work on segments of the newscast.

Reporters

Television reporters have to be quick on their feet. They spend a lot of time digging into stories, interviewing sources, and working with editors. Many television report-ers deliver the news on the air personally. Others provide information and material for the newscaster to deliver. And in many TV news situations, reporters have little time to get the information accurately and as completely and fairly as possible so that it can go on the air as it happens, ''live from the scene.''

Newscasters

Newscasters are more well known to us than most report-ers. These ''anchors,'' as they have become known, are personalities with whom viewers become familiar. Viewers develop loyalties to specific news programs be-cause they feel more comfortable with the newscaster, placing confidence in the news being delivered. These anchors include individuals who handle sports news and meteorologists who handle the weather.

Anchors, contrary to some viewpoints, are not just "pretty faces" who read the news. Most anchors are journalists who have worked hard as reporters and editors to get to their positions, which are premium jobs in television.

Specialists

Like newspapers, television has specialists who investigate, write, edit, and report news in such areas as education, health, entertainment, science, agriculture, and government, to name a few. People in these jobs usually have special education or backgrounds in these subjects that have been acquired over time. They also have worked their way through the ranks from beginning reporter. They may come from years covering a beat for a newspaper.

Photographers and Graphic Artists

Photography is a critical element for television. It is a visual medium. Photojournalists do more than point a camera and work with a sound person to record the events. They have creativity that allows them to attract attention by capturing the emotion and feelings that are part of the news, too. In some communities, photojournalists may also write, edit, and report the news. In other communities, they work with a team of people to produce the story.

At most television stations, photographers also are technicians. They set up microwave links from mobile trucks, for example.

Graphics are an equally important part of most television news operations. Artists work with computer graphics systems to create still and animated art and generate names and titles which are seen on the screen during newscasts.

Archivists

There is also another job often not thought about. The archivist keeps track of all tape and stories so that they can easily be updated when new developments occur, sometimes many months later.

It takes a lot of other people to produce television programs, such as camera operators, technical directors, make-up staff, sound technicians. When they aren't working on news, they are involved in other program activities of the station.

Regardless of the specific job an individual holds in either radio or television, broadcasting, like other media, requires teamwork. The anchor would be useless without news directors, managers, editors, reporters, camera and audio operators, switchers, floor directors, film and video editors photojournalists, news specialists, sportscasters, set designers, staging and lighting experts, the worldwide news wire and video networks—and a wide range of support staff, financial and administrative personnel and management. Broadcasting journalism offers challenge and excitement to the individual willing to work hard.

CHAPTER 6

MAGAZINE AND NEWSLETTER JOURNALISM CAREERS

Journalists can find plenty of challenge, excitement, and rewarding jobs working for magazines and newsletters. Thousands of magazines and newsletters are sold at newsstands, through subscriptions, or through the mail. With computer technology, there are even magazines and newsletters on–line, at home or office, for those who have a simple telephone hook–up and subscribe.

FEATURES OF MAGAZINES AND NEWSLETTERS

One feature of magazine and newsletter journalism is that many publications appeal to your special interests, hobbies, or other career areas. For example, you could work for a magazine for education professionals, combining an interest in education (or maybe even a teaching degree) with your journalistic skills. Or work for a magazine covering stories of interest about stamps, cats, orchids, religion, politics, restaurants, your city or state, farming, bluegrass music, investing, interior design, sewing, or one of hundreds of other subjects.

In addition to working on the major weekly news magazines that cover news events from around the world and maintain staffs or bureaus in key cities, many career opportunities exist for top-notch writers, editors, and photojournalists. In fact, it is estimated that more than twenty thousand magazines circulate in the United States alone. There are even magazines about magazines! Hundreds of new periodicals are started each year—and hundreds fold each year, too.

Think of the magazines you read. Why do you read them? They provide you with general news and information, or they provide you with information about an area of special interest. If they stop keeping you interested, you will stop buying them and shop for others.

To be successful, a periodical must understand the interests and information needs of its readers. As those interests change, the publication must change. Readers expect their magazines to be on the cutting edge for new information—a leadership role—in providing news. If they fail to change or lead, they can lose readers. Losing readers affects the amount of money for which advertising can be sold and could end the publication's life.

ORGANIZATION OF MAGAZINES
AND NEWSLETTERS

There are probably as many ways to draw organization charts for magazines and newsletters as there are publications. Smaller ones may have only two or three full-time employees, buying articles from free-lance writers or news services.

Free-lance writers are common in the magazine and newsletter business. A free-lancer is often self-employed and may write for a variety of publications. Or a free-lancer combines writing with another career or interest—a doctor who writes for medical magazines, or a teacher who writes for education publications. Stories a free-lancer writes are sold to an appropriate publication. You could even be free-lancing right now—writing articles about topics of special interest to you. (Check out *The Writer's Handbook,* edited by Sylvia K. Burack for The Writer, Inc. It is a guide to publications, telling you what types of stories they buy and how to sell them.)

Publisher

At the top of most periodical organization charts is a publisher—the person responsible for all departments of the publication, such as advertising, promotion, marketing and sales, circulation, and editorial. This job may be filled by someone who has a strong background in business or advertising, or someone who worked his or her way up through the editorial department. The publisher also could be the magazine's owner.

Editor

An editor or editor-in-chief, leads the editorial side of the publication that, depending again on size and scope, may be organized into subject or topical departments, in turn headed by department editors. The publication may have a staff of writers and editors, use a group of reliable free-lancers, or obtain articles from free-lancers who ''shop'' for publications to buy their work.

Regardless of the organizational structure and layers—or lack of layers—of titles, content is king. Magazines may offer a great opportunity for a career in journalism. And, like other careers, any journalism experience you can obtain through part-time jobs, internships, and formal college education is important. But with the variety of opportunities, individuals who have excellent backgrounds in a particular subject can take ''crash'' courses that will help them sharpen their writing skills for periodicals. Some of the courses are taught during summers, over weekends, or at night. Some courses are part of continuing education programs or correspondence classes. It also is important not to forget that free-lance writing can be done throughout another career—combining two or more important interests.

CHAPTER 7

JOURNALISM AND PUBLIC
RELATIONS CAREERS

As in magazines and newsletters, thousands of opportunities exist for you to combine an interest and ability in journalism with other areas of interest for a career in public relations.

WHERE PR PROFESSIONALS WORK

Today, public relations professionals work for school systems, colleges and universities, doctors and medical clinics, hospitals, governmental, social and community organizations, businesses, industry, professional associations and clubs, politicians and entertainers, to name a few.

Within the broad term public relations are specialty areas for careers, such as working with news media; coordinating community relations; writing, editing and managing newsletters, magazines and other publications for an organization; handling broadcast/video communications—script writing, editing, production and distribution; measuring public opinion; handling relationships with governmental officials—lobbying and public affairs; consumer relations; investor relations; marketing communications; issue management; speech writing; and managing special events.

Public relations is a two-way process of communications designed to build support, understanding, goodwill, and morale for a business, a person, a product, or an institution. A public relations professional develops a strategy that uses an array of communications techniques.

REQUIREMENTS FOR PR WORKERS

Public relations professionals more and more frequently come from news media backgrounds, or graduate from colleges and universities offering journalism/public relations degrees or programs.

Writing is the most important and critical skill required for effective public relations careers. Equally important are:

- the ability to develop effective strategies to use an array of communications tools and techniques to accomplish your organization's objectives;
- the ability to manage a number of activities effectively at one time.

- the quality of your personal communication and speaking skills;
- a strong knowledge of business and/or of the particular organization in which you work.

There is no better training around for public relations careers than working for a newspaper. You learn to sharpen your writing skills for a general readership. You'll be well prepared to ask hard questions and know how to do your homework for your readers. You will work under the pressure of deadlines.

In a public relations job you will need to be able to write effectively, translating complex or difficult information into terms an average person will understand—to bridge the communications gap between your organization and one or more of its audiences.

Accuracy, credibility and integrity are essential to being a successful public relations person. While you represent a point of view held by the organization you work for, media and others will respect you if you are a credible source. Be candid. Don't hide the bad news.

As part of your undergraduate education, take business courses. Most public relations jobs require a general understanding of business. Many professionals recommend a dual major or suggest that if you have an undergraduate degree in journalism, you obtain a master's degree in business. Many journalism graduates believe that their entire future will be working for the media. But far more journalism graduates will enter public relations careers over time than media. And, a background in business will be important for you to get the better jobs. Remember, journalists seldom write about journalism or public relations. You write about, or represent, the activities of business, organizations, and institutions.

CHAPTER 8

SUPPORTING CAREERS IN JOURNALISM

Some people like the excitement of the news media, but don't want to be writers, editors, or photographers. There are other careers that can be rewarding in media.

ADVERTISING

For example, it takes money to publish a newspaper, magazine, or newsletter, operate a broadcasting station, or maintain a public relations agency or department within an organization. Each of these organizations has advertising departments that sell, create, and provide advertising services. Without advertising, we would pay very high prices for the media we enjoy. This book isn't intended to discuss advertising opportunities. You will want to read *Opportunities in Advertising Careers,* by S. William Pattis; it is a companion book in the VGM Opportunities series and was published in 1988.

OFFICE SUPPORT

There are also secretaries, accountants, bookkeepers, and librarians (archivists). Someone has to coordinate and hire staff and manage the personnel functions, administering the payroll, benefits, and retirement programs of the organization.

MARKETING

There are also those who provide the marketing services and promotional activities for the media. For example, you see outdoor billboards, bus posters, hear advertisements on radio and read them in print publications promoting a particular television station or program. And media conduct their own programs for public relations benefits, such as crime stopper, health fairs, needy family drives, concerts, and other community service projects. Public relations is a job within many media businesses. So is advertising. The media would not survive without readers, listeners, and viewers.

TECHNOLOGISTS

Today's media rely heavily on technology. Media employ computer operators and programmers, experts on satellite technology, operators of sophisticated computer graphics equipment for such diverse uses as preparation of advertising, weather shows, simulations for news features, charts, and internal business reports.

Printers today operate precision machines that run much like computers, delivering just the right amount of various colors of ink to the pages you see.

CIRCULATION

And someone has to see that you buy and receive the products. Circulation of printed publications must take place throughout a wide market area. In the case of national newspapers and magazines, there may be regional printing facilities with vast trucking and mail networks to see that you have today's paper today.

With the rapid growth of cable television services has come a network of sales personnel, installers, and related business functions.

The news media are businesses. There are a lot of jobs that need to be filled by qualified men and women in order for the journalists to deliver their written products to the reader, listener, and viewer. If writing isn't your key interest, you can still have a rewarding career working with the media. It's exciting to be where the action is, helping people keep informed, entertained, educated, thinking. Helping stimulate the economy. Helping to keep government under public scrutiny. And, yes, helping shape the future by fairly and accurately delivering today's news to the public.

CHAPTER 9

PREPARING FOR A JOURNALISM CAREER

Let's say you've made your decision. You want to become a journalist.

You know the work is both rewarding and demanding. You know about the commitment you'll have to make. Still, you've decided journalism is for you.

Now what? How do you prepare for a journalism career?

PATHS TO SUCCESS

There's no easy answer, no one way to do it. Many paths can lead you to journalistic success.

A College Education

A question certain to come up early as you ponder what to do next concerns college. Is a college education required for a journalism career? Well, no, it's not *required* in the sense that a lawyer has to pass the Bar exam or in the sense that a pharmacist has to pass state exams to be licensed.

Many successful journalists passed up college and started their careers armed only with a high school diploma. A few even made it in journalism after dropping out of high school.

Notice the past tense here. The journalists just described tend to be older, and they began their careers in a different era. There is no question today: If you want to be a journalist, go to college. Examples of exceptions are too rare to count much in your decision-making.

Journalism Degree vs. Liberal Arts

The next question is more complex. Is a journalism degree necessary for a journalism career? Journalists, journalism professors, editors and station managers disagree widely. Here are the arguments.

Those who believe a journalism degree is *not* necessary argue that what a journalist needs most is a broad, liberal education. They say the study of history, economics, law, English, foreign languages, political science—the whole range of a liberal education—is more important than studying journalism.

The tricks of the journalistic trade, the argument goes, can be taught easily on the job. Journalism classes are a waste of time. Every journalism class taken is a history class *not* taken. Every minute spent working on a school newspaper is a minute *not* spent studying Shakespeare. Besides that, they argue, too many journalism professors are failed journalists who retreated to the campus because they couldn't make it in the "real world."

People who believe this advise would-be journalists to avoid journalism school and concentrate on becoming Renaissance men or women, truly well-educated people who can work effectively no matter what the subject matter of a story might be.

The other side of the story goes this way. To toss off journalism classes as merely passing along "tricks of the trade" is oversimplified. Journalism involves more than a few "tricks" that can be taught haphazardly in the newsroom, where there is little time for teaching anyway.

Journalism schools offer courses in mass media law, history, ethics, the role of the press in society. At its best, journalism education creates not just journalists but thoughtful journalists.

It's not enough merely to know how to write a story. A journalist must know why the story is being written (and sometimes when it's best *not* to write a story). Few working editors in a newsroom have time to coach young writers on the intricacies of newswriting, let alone law or ethics. The argument that you can learn journalism on the job is flawed because there is so little time on the job for teaching. It's true that the basics of newswriting, interviewing, and copy editing can be learned as you go. Still, there's much to be said for systematic learning. Journalism 201 follows Journalism 101 at a university. And where does the would-be journalist who never studied journalism learn press law? After the libel suit is filed?

As for journalism professors being failed journalists, who would deny that there's some truth to this? It's not so much "failed" as it is burnt-out. Indeed, some journalism profs teach because they got tired of the hard work of journalism, or of the odd hours or low pay. The majority, however, teach by choice, teach because teaching gives them joy and an opportunity to serve students and their craft. The best journalism professors have never *really* left journalism.

In the argument between journalism education and liberal arts, there's truth on both sides. One of the authors of this book worked five summers as adviser and writing instructor to a group of young journalists brought to Arizona for a journalism fellowship. They were all just out of college. Each was assigned a job at a newspaper but also learned through speakers, seminars, classes, and individual writing instruction. Participants in the program came from all sorts of educational backgrounds. Some were from small liberal arts schools. A few had Ivy League educations. Many came from important university journalism programs. A handful were picked from lesser-known journalism programs.

In assessing their performance, only one important pattern emerged. Successful participants were well-educated, whether in journalism or not. The ones with "J-schools" in their backgrounds knew the terminology better and got off to faster starts. What really mattered was the quality of their education. And a good education can be found at hundreds of universities.

If you decide to pursue a college education in journalism, you still must decide on which college. They're not all alike. In some ways, the arguments about journalism school vs. liberal arts are based on a false premise. There is no contradiction between going to a journalism school and getting a liberal education, provided you're careful about what school you pick and how you go about getting your education.

Accredited and Unaccredited Programs

If you pick an accredited university journalism program, you'll be *required* to concentrate on the liberal arts as well. The organization that accredits journalism schools insists that journalism majors take no more than one-fourth of their total credit hours in journalism. Thus, three-fourths must be devoted to liberal arts.

Some unaccredited journalism programs permit students to take a third or more of their units in journalism. Such programs do, indeed, undercut the notion of a liberal education. With all those units in journalism, what are you going to write about that you'll understand? Suppose you cover a speech and the speaker talks about supply-side economics. You took no economics because you were too busy taking every journalism class in the catalog, and your story makes no sense.

But even at an accredited school you can graduate basically uneducated if you do it wrong. Every journalism professor knows the pitfalls. If all you do in college is journalism, you're passing up much of your real education.

Getting Good Grades

Many journalism students overdo it. They devote all their time to their journalism classes or, more likely, to the school newspaper. They skip English classes, go infrequently to economics classes, pick the easiest foreign language and barely pass it. They graduate with a 2.1 grade point average (GPA) and wonder why they can't find a job.

School newspapers can provide wonderful experience for a journalism student. But not at the price of a 2.1 GPA.

Do grades count? Lots of people go through life with their 2.1 GPAs and never pay any penalties. Others graduate with 3.8 GPAs and never feel like they're rewarded for their effort. These are exceptions. Grades *do* count.

They count when the faculty votes on scholarships, when editors weigh the job applications of two otherwise-equal candidates with widely varying GPAs. They count when it's time to pass out honors and awards and when it's time to decide who gets into prestigious academic honorary societies. And they count if you want to go to graduate school.

Graduate School

Probably, if you're just now thinking about college, graduate school seems like a million miles away and something you haven't thought about anyway. Someday you might. What if you want to teach at the university level, for example? You'll need advanced degrees and you won't be able to get into graduate school without the grades. Most graduate schools require at least a 3.0, and many put the standard much higher than that.

More and more journalists are coming into the newsroom with master's degrees. A few even have Ph.D.'s. Law degrees are becoming more common, especially for people covering the judicial system.

Here most journalists agree: Advanced degrees are fine, especially if they add a speciality on top of a journalism degree. Many people, however, advise against getting *two* journalism degrees. If your undergraduate degree is in journalism, find a speciality to study in graduate school. If you have a liberal education from your undergraduate days, a master's in journalism might provide just the right amount of journalism schooling.

Picking a College

Picking a college can be difficult. Make sure you touch all the bases. Visit a guidance counselor. Request the college catalogs. Write the alumni association for graduates in your area and interview them.

If at all possible, however, your strategy should include a campus visit. You can learn a great deal about a journalism program by such a visit. For one thing, you can get an idea of how a program feels about students just by seeing how you're treated. Are you made to feel welcome? Is a faculty adviser available to see you?

Visit the school newspaper. If you want the *real* story about a journalism program, ask the students, not just the professors.

Make sure you find out the school's strengths and weaknesses. Some journalism schools put most of their effort and money into broadcasting. This would be no place for you if you want to go into print journalism. The reverse is true, of course. Steer clear of print-emphasis programs if your interests are in broadcasting.

OTHER LEARNING OPPORTUNITIES

Your quest to prepare yourself for a journalism career should include some other elements. Visit your local newspaper, broadcast station, or public relations firm. Ask the women and men there for advice. Most people are generous with their time when a young person wants advice. It's flattering for journalists to talk to someone who wants to be what they are. Ask these journalists how they prepared themselves. You'll find an array of paths.

In the meantime, become a student of journalism in your private world. Read newspapers, all you can get your hands on. Forget the tapes in your car: On the way to school or work, listen to National Public Radio. Watch a variety of TV newscasts and evaluate them. Make it a habit to read a variety of magazines. Go to your library and find the section on journalism.

Camp there.

CHAPTER 10

IS TEACHING FOR YOU?

Many people with urges to become journalists have other interests as well. A typical one, especially for someone just finishing high school, is teaching. After years of classroom work watching teachers in action, many young people develop an interest in teaching. This should not be discouraged at all.

Teaching is a rewarding life, but it's not without problems, of course. It is just that these problems aren't always readily visible to a student. Like professional journalists, teachers work long hours under sometimes difficult circumstances. Pay is too low, but as we said earlier, it is wrong to measure the satisfaction in a job by pay alone.

To see a student struggle with a concept for weeks and then to see the joy that comes when the concept is understood—well, money has nothing to do with that sort of reward.

But experienced teachers of today will tell you their jobs are becoming more difficult. You may have seen the surveys. Fifty years ago, teachers said their biggest problems had to do with students talking or chewing gum in class or sneaking a cigarette in the restrooms between classes. These problems seem pretty tame compared to what teachers face today. Drugs and alcohol, broken homes, pregnancies . . . today's students often face severe problems—and they bring them into the classroom.

Should you be a teacher? The qualities of successful teachers are many, but most people would agree that they share some traits. Number one, perhaps, is empathy, the ability to place yourself in the other person's position and therefore to understand that person. Good teachers have to be tough, of course, to maintain discipline and order in the classroom. But warmth, good humor, and patience are every bit as important as toughness.

If you want a career in teaching, you must prepare for it. In college, you will need a dual specialty. You need to take a journalism program as well as a teacher–preparation program through teacher's college or the education department. You have to learn to teach and learn something to teach.

In journalism, you probably ought to specialize in the news-editorial area, or print, in other words. Most schools still put more emphasis on the school newspaper than on broadcasting. You will need layout skills, not only for the newspaper but for the yearbook as well. Many journalism teachers advise both publications.

In addition, be aware of the fact that most teachers don't have the luxury of specializing in just one subject. In addition to journalism, you will need a specialty in some other area. Many journalism teachers also teach English. Assignments in history, social studies, or government are common.

Somewhere along the way in college, try to pick up some professional experience. Nothing enhances a teacher's credibility with students more than having real-world experience. It is one thing to teach from the book. It is quite another, and quite better, to teach from experience. Lacking long professional experience, it is still best to have some credentials as a working journalist.

Also while in college, make an absolute point of absorbing the rules of communications law. This means libel, invasion of privacy, obscenity, student press law. Lawsuits against school publications are rare but certainly something everyone on a publication should be concerned with. High school advisers have to know their own rights, the rights of their students, the rights of administrators. Deep trouble can await a teacher ignorant of journalism law.

Deep satisfaction, however, can be the other side of the coin. Committed teachers have good lives. Rewards are great in terms of watching students grow and develop. The ultimate thrill for a journalism teacher comes when a former student succeeds as a professional. That is hard to top.

CHAPTER 11

FINDING THAT FIRST JOB

Finding a job is work in itself. You may find yourself writing dozens of letters and making lots of phone calls before even getting an interview. If jobs aren't available, people often don't take the time to interview candidates. But that doesn't mean that you shouldn't try.

In fact, landing your first (and subsequent internships) requires the same process and plenty of effort. You have to sell yourself. Keep in mind that there are a lot of people looking for jobs. You need to give the individual interviewing you the reasons why you would be better than others who might apply.

WRITING A
COVER LETTER

The first step is to write a cover letter. Keep it to one page. Write it with great care. Remember, you are looking for a job where writing is the major tool of the trade. If your letter is poorly constructed, filled with spelling or grammatical errors, or uses improper punctuation, you can forget the phone call. It is always amazing to see, out of dozens of applications and resumes, how poorly people introduce themselves in writing. This is your first impression.

In your letter state briefly why you want to work for the employer, what you bring or offer. Give them a brief summary of relevant experience, if any. If not, be honest. Tell them you are looking for your first job—or internship. If you are willing to take an internship without pay, say that in the letter.

End the letter by stating that you will call in a few days to set an appointment. (Don't get ahead of yourself—give the post office time to deliver your letter before you call. But, at the same time, don't wait too long. You want to call soon after the letter arrives.)

What if you don't know who to write? Pick up the phone and call the media or prospective employer. After all, you are a journalist. Getting information is your career. It is not impressive to receive a job application addressed to a generic person.

YOUR RESUME

Enclose a well-constructed resume. One page. No, you don't need to have it printed. It should look neat, but employers are not hiring on superficial criteria. What the resume says is what is important.

At the top, type your full name, address, and phone number(s). The first section should state the position desired. For example:

> Position Desired: Unpaid news-related internship with opportunities to demonstrate writing capabilities and to learn more about a career in journalism.
>
> Position Desired: Beginning job on a newspaper copydesk.
>
> Position Desired: Beginning job with a public relations firm or agency in Denver, Colorado.

(If you have limiting criteria that affect where you can work, be sure to include it in your letter or resume. For example, if you will only accept paid positions as an intern or only work in Denver because a spouse or family member lives there, say so. There is no reason to spend time interviewing when there is no hope of getting—or taking—a job if it is offered.)

Next, summarize relevant experience. This should be done in a short paragraph. For example:

> Experience: Two summer internships at XYZ Press, working on copydesk, police reporting, selling classified ads.
>
> Sports editor, *The Buffalo,* West High School student newspaper.

Next follows a summary of your work career. As a student, or when seeking a first job, all jobs are important, even the one summer you spent sacking groceries. Here is a suggested format:

Work Experience:

> May 1990–September 1990—John's Grocery and Meat Market, sacking groceries, stocking shelves, cashier.
> September 1990–June 1991—Afterschool work at KXYZ Radio, handling phones, photocopying, storing archive audio tapes.

There are those who suggest you list your experience chronologically. Others suggest you start with the most current job, then go backward to show the growth in responsibilities and what you did most recently. The choice is yours.

Then you will follow with "education." List the places you went to school, starting with high school, and degree earned or last year completed, with the years of attendance.

"Extracurricular activities" will be important in early job applications. Later, you will include your community involvements. Include memberships and affiliations, especially those that could be relevant to the job you seek.

Any honors, awards, scholarships? They are important. List those next.

Next, provide a page with the names, addresses, and phone numbers for three to five references. It helps to indicate how you know each one. For example: Steven Smith, supervisor at KXYZ Radio. This helps the prospective employer understand how the individual can best answer questions about you.

Once again, be sure you check for spelling, grammar, and punctuation. There are a lot of employers who will circle any typo or spelling error and ask to have a reject letter sent.

CHAPTER 12

SOME BOOKS YOU SHOULD READ

An almost countless number of books have been written about journalism and subjects related to it. Cutting that number to this small list of suggested readings was no easy task. Students and others considering journalism as a career should not limit their reading to this list. But anyone who reads every book suggested here will be on his or her way to an understanding of the field.

TEXTBOOKS

Dozens of survey texts have been written for use in high school and college classes. These texts touch on every journalistic topic. The one we recommend is virtually the standard in the field. It's *Introduction to Mass Communications* by Agee, Ault and Emery (New York: Harper & Row, 1989). The book has been around a long time (it's now in its ninth edition). The authors and their publishers keep the book completely up-to-date, constantly incorporating information about new technologies and other mass media developments. Journalism's growth and development are thoroughly explored, with chapters on newspapers, news services and syndicates, magazines, book publishing, radio, television, and even recordings. Other chapters provide information on the role of the press and its impact in society, tracing various mass communications theories. In "The Persuasive Professions," the authors describe the role of advertising and public relations. They close with criticisms and challenges of the media. The book is almost encyclopedic. Persons interested in a career in journalism or fields related to it will find a thorough explanation of that field.

A similar work is *Media/Reader: Perspectives on Mass Media Industries, Effects, and Issues* by Shirley Biagi of California State University, Sacramento (Belmont, Calif.: Wadsworth Publishing Co., 1989). Basically, a reader is a collection of related essays touching on a variety of current topics. Professor Biagi's book runs the gamut from an article by a woman police reporter discussing the homocides she's covered to scholarly as well as popularized looks at media effects and the legal and regulatory issues facing the media. Because of the wide variety of writers, issues and writing styles, *Media/Reader* is easier reading than *Introduction to Mass Communications* though both explore many of the same issues. Professor Biagi is careful to give equal space to all sides of the various difficult media issues.

The next book we recommend is actually a series of books. Each year the Modern Media Institute in St. Petersburg, Fla., reproduces in book form the winning entries in the American Society of Newspaper Editors, writing and reporting competitions. The series started with *Best Newspaper Writing 1979* and has continued since. Any book in the series would be valuable reading for someone wanting to see the best work of American newspaper journalists. Some of the writing is breathtaking. Not only are the winning articles reproduced, but their authors are interviewed on how they gathered and wrote their stories. These interviews constitute virtually a college–level course in writing and reporting. The books are available from The Poynter Institute for Media Studies, Post Office Box 31266, St. Petersburg, Fla.

ON INTERVIEWING

The art of the interview has occupied many journalistic authors. None has produced a more thorough, interesting, and readable book about interviewing that Killenberg and Anderson, authors of *Before the Story: Interviewing and Communication Skills for Journalists* (New York: St. Martin's Press, 1989). Many interviewing guides are simply tips offered by journalists. This book, however, is thoroughly grounded in communications theory and explores why interviews work and don't work. An extensive bibliography provides good suggestions for further reading.

The research and theoretical underpinnings certainly show through in this book, but the writing style and anecdotal material make it a readable and enjoyable work.

WRITING ABOUT WRITING

Columnist James Kilpatrick arouses various emotions when he writes about politics from his conservative viewpoint. However, when he writes about writing, the verdict is unanimous: His words about words need to be taken seriously. In *The Writer's Art* (Kansas City, Andrews, McMeel & Parker Inc., 1984), Kilpatrick takes the reader on a guided tour of what's good and bad about American English usage. Writing, as we have noted, is the journalist's fundamental skill. Anyone interested in improving his or her writing will profit from a close reading, and re-reading, of this book. Kilpatrick is occasionally sarcastic and sharp-tongued, but he always has something to say, and he says it interestingly. If you're serious enough to want to know the distinctions between such words as flaunt and flout, flotsam and jetsam, disinterested and uninterested, envy and jealousy—and many others—here's where to look. TV journalist Edwin Newman and columnist William Safire have similiar books. All are recommended.

And here is a gem, perhaps the best book ever written about writing. It's *On Writing Well: An Informal Guide to*

Writing Nonfiction by William Zinsser (New York: Harper & Row, 1988. You can read this book in half a day. Take it seriously and it can change your life as a writer. First, it's a perfect example of everything it preaches: simple, uncluttered, clear, witty, concise. It's filled with examples, good and bad, that everyone who writes can relate to. Most journalists are more familiar with another small book on writing, Strunk & White's *Elements of Style*. *Elements of Style* should be on every writer's shelf. If you can have only one, however, make it *On Writing Well*.

BOOKS ABOUT PUBLIC RELATIONS

There is one book in public relations you should read. It is a collection of short chapters on nearly every aspect of public relations, each written by an expert practitioner. You will get an insight into the field and its diversity. *Experts in Action—Inside Public Relations* by Cantor, Bill (White Plains, N.Y., Longman, Inc., 1989).

Another useful book is the leading text used at colleges and universities by beginning public relations students. *Effective Public Relations* by Cutlip, Center and Broom (Englewood Cliffs, N.J., Prentice-Hall, Inc.) It takes you through the nuts and bolts of each phase of the public relations process and applications.

ADVICE FROM WINNERS

Karen Rothmyer's book *Winning Pulitzers* (New York, N.Y., Columbia University Press) lets Pulitzer Prize winners tell in their own words how they got their stories. The book also chronicles the changes that have occurred in journalism since the prizes were begun. One prize winner said the award ''was as if the Supreme Court of our own profession had ruled in our favor.'' But another said the prize has been something of a burden. She wrote, ''It makes you feel you have an awful lot to live up to. Since I won I've even found myself writing two drafts of personal letters.''

APPENDIX A

CAREER RESOURCES

As you study career opportunities in journalism, you will want to read other books in the VGM Career Horizons series. Specifically, look for:

Pattis, S. William. *Opportunities in Advertising Careers.* Lincolnwood, Ill.: VGM Career Horizons, 1988.

Ellis, Elmo I. *Opportunities in Broadcasting Careers.* Lincolnwood, Ill.: VGM Career Horizons, 1986.

Pattis, S. William. *Opportunities in Magazine Publishing Careers.* Lincolnwood, Ill.: VGM Career Horizons, 1986.

Rotman, Morris B. *Opportunities in Public Relations Careers.* Lincolnwood, Ill.: VGM Career Horizons, 1988.

You may want to write for information from:

American Association of
    Advertising Agencies, Inc.
666 Third Avenue
New York, N.Y. 10017
*Advertising: A Guide to
    Careers in Advertising.*
Send $1.

Advertising Education
    Publications
623 Meadow Bend Dr.
Baton Rouge, La. 70808.
*Where Should I Go To College
To Study Journalism?* Send
$2.

American Society of Newspaper
    Editors Foundation
P. O. Box 17004
Washington, D.C. 20041.
Free Resource Bulletin.

Bureau of Education and
    Research
American Advertising
    Federation
400 K Street, N.W.
Washington, D.C. 20005.
Jobs in Advertising. Send $.75
and self-addressed envelope.

The Canadian Association of
    Broadcasters
P. O. Box 627, Stn. B.
Ottawa, Canada, KIP 552.
Careers in Broadcasting.

Radio Television News Directors
    Association
1735 DeSales Street, N.W.
Washington, D.C. 20036.
Careers in Broadcast News.
Send self-addressed, 6 x 9
envelope with $.45 postage.

National Association of
    Broadcasters, Publications
    Department
1771 N Street, N.W.
Washington, D.C. 20036.
Careers in Radio and *Careers
in Television.* Send $2 for
each.

National Cable Television
    Association
1724 Massachusetts Ave.
Washington, D.C. 20036.
Careers in Cable. Send $3.50.

National Newspaper Foundation
1627 K Street, N.W.
Washington, D.C. 20006.
*Journalism: Your Newspaper
Career and How to Prepare
for It.* Also, *Your Newspaper
Career.*

American Newspaper Publishers
    Association Foundation
The Newspaper Center, Box
    17407
Dulles International Airport
Washington, D.C. 20041.
Newspapers—Your Future?
    Also, *The Newspaper:
    What's In It For Me?*

National Press Photographers
    Association, Inc.
3200 Crousdale Dr. #306
Durham, N.C. 27705.
Careers in News Photography.

Public Relations Society of
    America, Inc.
33 Irving St.
New York, N.Y. 10013.
Careers in Public Relations.
    Send $1.

Dow Jones Newspaper Fund
    P. O. Box 300
    Princeton, N.J. 08543.
    *Minority Journalism Career
    Guide.*

Women In Communications
    P. O. Box 17460
    Arlington, Va. 22216.
    Careers in Communications.

Women in Radio and Television,
    Inc.
    11101 Connecticut Ave.,
    N.W., No. 700.
    Washington, D.C. 20041.
    Careers in Electronic Media.
    Free.

COLLEGES AND UNIVERSITIES OFFERING JOURNALISM PROGRAMS

Following is a listing of colleges and universities in the United States and Canada that offer courses or degree programs in journalism. Contact them for course descriptions and specific details on programs offered. Many community and junior colleges also offer courses in journalism. While they are not included here, you may want to contact those institutions near you.

Alabama

Alabama State University
Department of
Communications Media
Montgomery, AL
36195-0301

Auburn University
Department of Journalism
Auburn, AL 36830

Samford University
Department of
Journalism–Mass
Communications
Birmingham, AL 35229

Troy State University
Hall School of Journalism
Troy, AL 36082

University of Alabama
    College of Communication
    Box 870172
    Tuscaloosa, AL
    35487-0172

Alaska

University of Alaska at
    Anchorage
    3211 Providence Dr.
    Department of Journalism
    and Public
    Communications
    Anchorage, AK 99508

University of
    Alaska–Fairbanks
    Department of Journalism
    and Broadcasting
    Fairbanks, AK 99775-0940

Arizona

Arizona State University
    Walter Cronkite School of
    Journalism and
    Telecommunications
    Tempe, AZ 85287-1305

Northern Arizona University
    School of Communications
    Box 5619
    Flagstaff, AZ 86011

University of Arizona
    Department of Journalism
    Tucson, AZ 85721

Arkansas

Arkansas State University
    College of Communications
    Box 24
    State University, AR 72467

Arkansas Tech University
    Department of Speech,
    Theatre and Journalism
    Russellville, AR 72801

Harding University
    Department of
    Communication
    Searcy, AR 72143

Henderson State
    University
    Department of
    Communication Arts
    and Sciences
    Arkadelphia, AR 71923

John Brown University
Department of Journalism
Siloam Springs, AR 72761

Ouachita Baptist University
Department of
Communications
Arkadelphia, AR 71923

University of Arkansas,
Fayetteville
Department of Journalism
Fayetteville, AR 72701

University of Arkansas, Little
Rock
Department of Journalism
2801 South University
Little Rock, AR 72204

University of Central Arkansas
Department of Speech,
Theatre and Journalism
Conway, AR 72032

California

California Polytechnic State
University
Journalism Department
San Luis Obispo, CA
93407

California State Polytechnic
University at Pomona
Communication Arts
Department
Pomona, CA 91768

California State University

—Chico
School of Communications
Chico, CA 95929

—Dominquez Hills
Communications
Department
Carson, CA 90747

—Fresno
Department of Journalism
Fresno, CA 93740

—Fullerton
Department of
Communications
Fullerton, CA 92634

—Hayward
Department of Mass
Communication
Hayward, CA 94542

—Long Beach
Department of Journalism
Long Beach, CA 90840

—Los Angeles
Department of
Communications Studies
Los Angeles, CA 90032

—Northridge
Department of Journalism
Northridge, CA 91330

—Sacramento
Department of Journalism
Sacramento, CA 95819

Humboldt State University
Department of Journalism
Arcata, CA 95521

Menlo College
Mass Communications
Department
Atherton, CA 94025

Pacific Union College
Communication Department
Angwin, CA 94508

Pepperdine University
Seaver College
Communication Division
Malibu, CA 90263

San Diego State University
Department of Journalism
San Diego, CA 92182

San Francisco State University
Department of Journalism
San Francisco, CA 94132

San Jose State University
Department of Journalism
and Mass
Communications
San Jose, CA 95192

Santa Clara University
Department of
Communications
St. Joseph 209
Santa Clara, CA 95053

Stanford University
Department of
Communications
Stanford, CA 94305

University of California at
Berkeley
Graduate School of
Journalism
Berkeley, CA 94720

University of La Verne
Department of
Communications
La Verne, CA 91750

University of Southern
California
School of Journalism
Los Angeles, CA 90089

University of the Pacific
Department of
Communication
Stockton, CA 95211

University of San Francisco
Communications Arts
Department
2130 Fulton St.
San Francisco, CA 94117

Colorado

Adams State College
Communications
Department
Alamosa, CO 81102

Colorado State University
Department of Technical
Journalism
Fort Collins, CO 80523

Metro State College
Department of Journalism
1006 11th Street
Denver, CO 80204

University of Colorado
School of Journalism
Boulder, CO 80309

University of Denver
Department of Mass
Communications
Denver, CO 80208

University of Northern
Colorado
Department of Journalism
and Mass
Communications
Greeley, CO 80639

University of Southern
Colorado
Department of Mass
Communications
Pueblo, CO 81001

Connecticut

Southern Connecticut State
University
Journalism Department
New Haven, CT 06515

University of Bridgeport
Department of Mass
Communication
Bridgeport, CT 06601

University of Connecticut
Journalism Department
Storrs, CT 06268

University of Hartford
Communications
Department
West Hartford, CT 06117

University of New Haven
Department of
Communications
and Marketing
West Haven, CT 06516

Mount Vernon College
Communications
Department
Washington, DC 20007

Florida

Delaware

University of Delaware
Journalism Program
Newark, DE 19716

Florida A&M University
School of Journalism,
Media and Graphic Arts
Tallahassee, FL 32307

Florida International
University
Department of
Communication
North Miami, FL 33181

District of Columbia

The American University
School of Communication
4400 Massachusetts Ave.,
N.W.
Washington, DC 20016

Florida Southern College
Communications
Department
111 Lake Hollingsworth Dr.
Lakeland, FL 33801

George Washington University
Journalism Department
Washington, DC 20052

Howard University
Department of
Journalism
Washington, DC 20059

Jacksonville University
Department of Mass
Communication Studies
Jacksonville, FL 32211

University of Central Florida
Department of
Communication
Orlando, FL 32816

University of Florida
  College of Journalism &
  Communications
  Gainesville, FL 32611

University of Miami
  School of Communication
  Box 248127
  Coral Gables, FL 33124

University of North Florida
  Department of Language
  and Literature
  Program in
  Communications
  Jacksonville, FL 32216

University of South
  Florida
  Department of Mass
  Communications
  Tampa, FL 33620

University of West Florida
  Communication Arts
  Pensacola, FL 32514

Georgia

Brenau College
  Department of Humanities
  and Communication Arts
  Gainsville, GA 30501

Clark Atlanta University
  Mass Communications
  Department
  Atlanta, GA 30314

Georgia Southern College
  Journalism Program
  Department of
  Communication Arts
  Statesboro, GA 30460

Georgia State University
  Department of
  Communication
  Atlanta, GA 30303

Mercer University at Macon
  Communication
  Concentration Program
  Macon, GA 31207

Savannah State College
  State College Branch
  Department of Mass
  Communications
  Savannah, GA 31404

University of Georgia
  Henry W. Grady School of
  Journalism and Mass
  Communications
  Athens, GA 30602

Hawaii

University of Hawaii at Manda
Department of Journalism
Honolulu, HI 96822

Idaho

Boise State University
Department of
Communication
Boise, ID 83725

Idaho State University
Department of Mass
Communication
Pocatello, ID 83209

University of Idaho
School of Communication
Moscow, ID 83843

Illinois

Bradley University
Division of Communication
Peoria, IL 61625

College of St. Francis
Department of Journalism/
Communications
Joliet, IL 60435

Columbia College Chicago
Department of Journalism
600 South Michigan Ave.
Chicago, IL 60605

DePaul University
Department of English and
Communication
Chicago, IL 60614

Eastern Illinois University
Department of Journalism
Charleston, IL 61920

Illinois State University
Mass Communication
Program
Normal, IL 61701

Lewis University
Department of
Communications-
Theater
Romeoville, IL 60441

Loyola University of Chicago
Department of
Communication
Chicago, IL 60611

MacMurray College
Journalism Program
Jacksonville, IL 62650

Northern Illinois University
Department of Journalism
DeKalb, IL 60115

Northwestern University
Medill School of
Journalism
Evanston, IL 60201

Roosevelt University
Department of Journalism
Chicago, IL 60605

Southern Illinois University,
Carbondale
School of Journalism
Carbondale, IL 62901

Southern Illinois University,
Edwardsville
Department of Mass
Communications
Edwardsville, IL 62026

Western Illinois University
Department of English &
Journalism
Macomb, IL 61455

University of Illinois
College of Communications
Urbana, IL 61801

Indiana

Anderson College
Department of
Communications
Anderson, IN 46012

Ball State University
Department of Journalism
Muncie, IN 47306

Butler University
Department of Journalism
4600 Sunset Ave.
Indianapolis, IN 46208

Calumet College
Division of
Communication and
Fine Arts
Whiting, IN 46394

DePauw University
Department of
Communication Arts
and Sciences
Greencastle, IN 46135

Franklin College
Pulliam School of
Journalism
Franklin, IN 46131

Goshen College
  Department of
    Communication
  Goshen, IN 46526

Indiana State University
  Department of
    Communication
  Terre Haute, IN 47809

Indiana University
  School of Journalism
  Bloomington, IN 47405

Indiana University
  School of Journalism
  Indianapolis, IN 46202

Purdue University
  Department of
    Communication
  West Lafayette, IN 47907

St. Mary–of–the–Woods
    College
  Journalism Department
  St. Mary–of–the–Woods,
    IN 47876

Valparaiso University
  Department of
    Communications
  Valparaiso, IN 46383

Vincennes University
  The Journalism Program
  Vincennes, IN 47591

University of Evansville
  Department of
    Communication
  Evansville, IN 47702

University of Notre Dame
  Department of American
    Studies
  Journalism Program
  Notre Dame, IN 46556

Iowa

Clarke College
  Communication Department
  Dubuque, IA 52001

Drake University
  School of Journalism and
    Mass Communication
  Des Moines, IA 50311

Grand View College
  Communication Department
  Des Moines, IA 50316

Iowa State University
  Department of Journalism
    and Mass
    Communication
  Ames, IA 50011

Marycrest College
Department of
Communications and
Performing Arts
Davenport, IA 52804

University of Iowa
School of Journalism and
Mass Communication
Iowa City, IA 52242

University of Northern Iowa
Department of English
Journalism Program
Cedar Falls, IA 50614

Kansas

Baker University
Department of
Communication
Baldwin City, KS 66006

Benedictine College
Department of
Journalism/Mass
Communications
Atchison, KS 66002

Fort Hays State University
Department of
Communications
Hays, KS 67601

Kansas State University
Department of Journalism
and Mass
Communications
Manhattan, KS 66506

St. Mary of the Plains College
Department of Journalism
Dodge City, KS 67801

Pittsburg State University
Department of
Communication
Pittsburg, KS 66762

University of Western Kansas
Department of
Communication
Hays, KS 67601

University of Kansas
William Allen White
School of Journalism
Lawrence, KS 66045

Washburn University
Center for Media and
Communication Studies
Topeka, KS 66621

Wichita State University
Department of Journalism
Wichita, KS 67208

Kentucky

Eastern Kentucky
University
Department of Mass
Communications
Richmond, KY 40475

Morehead State
University
Journalism Area
Morehead, KY 40351

Murray State University
Department of Journalism
and Radio-TV
Murray, KY 42071

Northern Kentucky University
Department of
Communication
Highland Heights, KY
41076

University of Kentucky
School of Journalism
Lexington, KY 40506

University of Louisville
Department of
Communication
Louisville, KY 40202

Western Kentucky
University
Department of Journalism
Bowling Green, KY 42101

Louisiana

Grambling State University
Department of
English/Journalism
Grambling, LA 71245

Louisiana State University
School of Journalism
Baton Rouge, LA 70803

Louisiana State University in
Shreveport
Department of
Communications
Shreveport, LA 71115

Louisiana Tech University
Journalism Department
Ruston, LA 71272

Loyola University of the South
Department of
Communications
New Orleans, LA 70118

Nicholls State University
  Communication Arts
    Program
  Thibodaux, LA 70301

Northeast Louisiana University
  Department of
    Communication Arts
  Monroe, LA 71209

Northwestern State University
    of Louisiana
  Division of Journalism
  Nachitoches, LA 71497

Southeastern Louisiana
    University
  Department of English
  Hammond, LA 70402

University of New Orleans
  Journalism Area
  New Orleans, LA 70148

University of Southwestern
    Louisiana
  Journalism Program
  Lafayette, LA 70504

Xavier University of Louisiana
  Mass Communications
    Department
  New Orleans, LA 70125

Maine

University of Maine at Orono
  Department of Journalism
    and Broadcasting
  Orono, ME 04469

Maryland

Bowie State College
  Department of
    Communications
  Bowie, MD 20715

Loyola College
  Writing and Media
    Department
  Baltimore, MD 21210

Towson State University
  Journalism Program
  Baltimore, MD 21204

University of Maryland
  College of Journalism
  College Park, MD 20742

Massachusetts

Boston University
    College of Communication
    Boston, MA 02215

Emerson College
    Mass Communication
        Division
    Boston, MA 02116

Hampshire College
    School of Communications
        and Cognitive Science
    Amherst, MA 01002

Northeastern University
    Department of Journalism
    Boston, MA 02115

Simmons College
    Department of
        Communications
    Boston, MA 02115

Suffolk University
    Department of Journalism
    Boston, MA 02108

University of Massachusetts
    Journalistic Studies
    Amherst, MA 01003

Michigan

Alma College
    Journalism Program
    Alma, MI 48801

Central Michigan University
    Department of Journalism
    Mt. Pleasant, MI 48859

Eastern Michigan University
    Department of English
        Language and Literature
    Ypsilanti, MI 48197

Grand Valley State College
    School of Communications
    Allendale, MI 49401

Madonna College
    Journalism-Public
        Relations Program
    Livonia, MI 48150

Michigan State University
    School of Journalism
    East Lansing, MI 48824

Oakland University
    Journalism Program
    Rochester, MI 48309

University of Detroit
    Communications Studies
        Department
    Detroit, MI 48122

University of Michigan
Department of
Communication
Ann Arbor, MI 48109

Wayne State University
Journalism Area
Detroit, MI 48202

Western Michigan
University
Journalism Program
Kalamazoo, MI 49008

Minnesota

Bemidji State University
Journalism Program
Bemidji, MN 56601

College of St. Thomas
Department of Journalism
and Mass
Communications
St. Paul, MN 55105

Mankato State University
Mass Communications
Institute
Mankato, MN 56001

Morehead State University
Mass Communications
Department
Morehead, MN 56560

St. Cloud State University
Department of Mass
Communications
St. Cloud, MN 56301

St. Mary's College
Journalism & Mass
Communication
Department
Winona, MN 55987

University of Minnesota
School of Journalism and
Mass Communication
Minneapolis, MN 55455

University of Minnesota
Department of Agricultural
Journalism
St. Paul, MN 55108

Winona State University
Department of Mass
Communication
Winona, MN 55987

Mississippi

Jackson State University
Department of Mass
Communications
Jackson, MS 39217

Rust College
Department of Mass
Communications
Holly Springs, MS 38635

Mississippi State
University
Department of
Communication
Mississippi State, MS
39762

Mississippi University
for Women
Department of
Communication
Columbus, MS 39701

University of Southern
Mississippi
Department of Journalism
Hattiesburg, MS 39406

Tougaloo College
Journalism Program
Tougaloo, MS 39174

University of Mississippi
Department of Journalism
University, MS 39217

Missouri

Central Missouri State
University
Department of
Communication
Warrensburg, MO 64093

Culver-Stockton College
Department of Journalism
Canton, MO 63435

Evangel College
Department of
Communication
Springfield, MO 65802

Lincoln University
Department of
Communications
Jefferson City, MO 65101

Lindenwood College
Communications
Department
St. Charles, MO 63301

Maryville College
  Department of
  Communications
  St. Louis, MO 63141

Missouri Western State
  College
  Department of
  Journalism
  St. Joseph, MO 64507

Northeast Missouri State
  University
  Mass Communications
  Department
  Kirksville, MO 63501

Northwest Missouri State
  University
  Department of Mass
  Communication
  Maryville, MO 64468

St. Louis University
  Journalism Program
  St. Louis, MO 63108

Southeast Missouri State
  University
  Department of Mass
  Communications
  Cape Girardeau, MO 63701

Stephens College
  Communications
  Department
  Columbia, MO 65215

University of Missouri
  School of Journalism
  Columbia, MO 65205

University of Missouri–St.
  Louis
  Mass Communication
  Program
  St. Louis, MO 63121

Webster College
  Department of Journalism
  St. Louis, MO 63119

Montana

University of Montana
  School of Journalism
  Missoula, MT 59812

Nebraska

Creighton University
  Department of
  Journalism
  and Mass
  Communication
  Omaha, NE 68178

Hastings College
Communications Arts
Department
Hastings, NE 68901

Kearney State College
Department of
Journalism
Kearney, NE 68849

University of Nebraska–
Lincoln
College of Journalism
Lincoln, NE 68588

University of Nebraska–
Omaha
Department of
Communication
Omaha, NE 68182

Nevada

University of Las Vegas,
Nevada
Department of
Communication
Studies
Las Vegas, NV 89154

University of Nevada, Reno
Reynolds School of
Journalism
Reno, NV 89557

New Hampshire

Keene State College
Journalism Program
Keene, NH 03431

University of New Hampshire
Journalism Program
Durham, NH 03824

New Jersey

Fairleigh Dickinson University
Department of
Communications
Teaneck, NJ 07666

Glassboro State College
Communications
Department
Glassboro, NJ 08028

Rider College
Department of
Communications
Lawrenceville, NJ 08648

Rutgers University
Department of Journalism
and Mass Media
New Brunswick, NJ 08903

Seton Hall University
Department of
Communications
South Orange, NJ 07079

New Mexico

Eastern New Mexico
University
Department of
Communicative Arts
and Sciences
Portales, NM 88130

New Mexico Highlands
University
Department of Journalism
Las Vegas, NM 87701

New Mexico State
University
Department of
Journalism and Mass
Communications
Las Cruces, NM 88003

University of New Mexico
Department of Journalism
Albuquerque, NM 87131

New York

Albany State University of
New York
Department of English
Albany, NY 12222

Canisius College
Department of
Communication
Buffalo, NY 14208

College of New Rochelle
Communications Arts
Department
New Rochelle, NY 10805

College of White Plains
Pace University
White Plains, NY 10603

Columbia University
Graduate School of
Journalism
New York, NY 10027

Cornell University
Department of
Communication
Ithaca, NY 14853

Empire State College of
S.U.N.Y.
Journalism Program
Rochester, NY 14607

Fordham University
Department of
Communications
Bronx, NY 10458

Hofstra University
Communication Arts
Department
Hampstead, NY 11550

Iona College
Department of
Communication Arts
New Rochelle, NY 10801

Long Island University
Department of Journalism
Brooklyn, NY 11201

Marist College
Division of Arts and Letters
Lowell Thomas
Communications
Center
Poughkeepsie, NY 12601

New York University
Department of Journalism
and Mass
Communications
New York, NY 10003

Niagara University
Communication Studies
Program
Niagara University, NY
14109

Rochester Institute of
Technology
Photojournalism
Department
Rochester, NY 14623

St. Bonaventure University
Department of Mass
Communication
St. Bonaventure, NY 14778

St. John Fisher College
Communication/
Journalism
Rochester, NY 14618

State University College at
Buffalo
Department of Journalism,
Broadcasting and Speech
Buffalo, NY 14222

Syracuse University
Newhouse School of Public
Communications
Syracuse, NY 13210

Utica College of Syracuse
University
Department of Journalism
and Public Relations
Utica, NY 13502

North Carolina

Appalachian State University
Department of
Communication Arts
Boone, NC 28608

East Carolina University
Journalism Program
Greenville, NC 27834

Elon College
Journalism-Mass
Communication
Department
Elon College, NC 27244

Johnson C. Smith University
Department of
Communication Arts
Charlotte, NC 28216

University of North Carolina
School of Journalism
Chapel Hill, NC 27514

University of North
Carolina–Asheville
Communications Program
Asheville, NC 28804

Wingate College
Communication Studies
Wingate, NC 28174

North Dakota

North Dakota State University
Department of Mass
Communication
Fargo, ND 58105

University of North
Dakota
School of Communication
Grand Forks, ND 58202

Ohio

Bowling Green State
University
Department of Journalism
Bowling Green, OH 43403

Cleveland State
University
Department of
Communication
Cleveland, OH 44115

Kent State University
School of Journalism
Kent, OH 44242

Marietta College
Mass Media Department
Marietta, OH 45750

Ohio State University
   School of Journalism
   Columbus, OH 43210

Ohio University
   E. W. Scripps School of
     Journalism
   Athens, OH 45701

Ohio Wesleyan University
   Department of Journalism
   Delaware, OH 43015

Otterbein College
   Journalism Program
   Westerville, OH 43081

University of Akron
   Department of
     Communication
   Akron, OH 44325

University of Cincinnati
   Department of English
   Cincinnati, OH 45221

University of Dayton
   Department of
     Communication
   Dayton, OH 45469

University of Toledo
   Department of
     Communication
   Toledo, OH 43606

Wright State University
   Department of
     Communication
   Dayton, OH 45435

Oklahoma

Bethany Nazarene College
   Mass Communications
   Bethany, OK 73008

Central State University
   Journalism Department
   Edmond, OK 73034

East Central University
   Communications
     Department
   Ada, OK 74820

Northeastern State
     University
   Department of
     Journalism
   Tehlequah, OK 74464

Oklahoma Baptist
     University
   Department of Journalism
   Shawnee, OK 74801

Oklahoma City University
Department of Mass
Communications
Oklahoma City, OK 73106

Oklahoma State University
School of Journalism and
Broadcasting
Stillwater, OK 74078

University of Oklahoma
H. H. Herbert School of
Journalism and Mass
Communication
Norman, OK 73019

University of Tulsa
Faculty of Communication
Tulsa, OK 74104

Oregon

Linfield College
Department of
Communications
McMinnville, OR 97128

Oregon State University
Department of Journalism
Corvallis, OR 97331

Southern Oregon State
University
Department of
Communication
Ashland, OR 97520

University of Oregon
School of Journalism
Eugene, OR 97403

Pennsylvania

Bloomsburg University
Department of Mass
Communications
Bloomsburg, PA 17815

Cabrini College
Department of English and
Communications
Radnor, PA 19087

Duquesne University
Department of
Journalism
Pittsburgh, PA 15282

Elizabeth College
Department of
Communications
Elizabethtown, PA 17022

Indiana University of
Pennsylvania
Department of Journalism
Indiana, PA 15705

Lehigh University
Division of Journalism
Bethlehem, PA 18015

Point Park College
Department of Journalism
and Communications
Pittsburgh, PA 15222

Shippensburg University
Communications/
Journalism
Department
Shippensburg, PA 17257

Temple University
Department of Journalism
Philadelphia, PA 19122

The Pennsylvania
State University
School of Communication
University Park, PA 16802

University of Pittsburgh
Department of English
Pittsburgh, PA 15260

Rhode Island

University of Rhode Island
Department of Journalism
Kingston, RI 02881

South Carolina

Benedict College
Journalism Program
Columbia, SC 29204

University of South
Carolina
College of Journalism
Columbia, SC 29208

Winthrop College
Department of
Communications
Rock Hill, SC 29733

South Dakota

Black Hills State University
Communications
Division
Spearfish, SD 57783

Mount Marty College
Journalism Program
Yankton, SD 57078

South Dakota State University
Department of Journalism
and Mass
Communication
Brookings, SD 57007

University of South Dakota
Mass Communications,
Journalism Department
Vermillion, SD 57069

Tennessee

Austin Peay State
University
Communication Arts Major
Clarksville, TN 37044

Christian Brothers
College
Journalism Option
Memphis, TN 38104

Tennessee Technological
University
Journalism Curriculum
Cookeville, TN 38505

University of Tennessee
at Chattanooga
Communications
Department
Chattanooga, TN 37402

University of Tennessee at
Martin
Department of
Communications
Martin, TN 38238

Texas

Abilene Christian
University
Journalism and Mass
Communication
Department
Abilene, TX 79699

Angelo State University
Department of
Journalism
San Angelo, TX 76909

Baylor University
Department of Journalism
Waco, TX 76798

East Texas State
    University
    Journalism and
    Graphic Arts Department
    Commerce, TX 75428

Hardin-Simmons University
    Department of
    Communication
    Abilene, TX 79698

Howard Payne University
    Department of
    Communications
    Brownwood, TX 76801

Midwestern State University
    Journalism Program
    Wichita Falls, TX 76308

North Texas State
    University
    Department of
    Journalism
    Denton, TX 76201

Pan American
    University
    Communications
    Department
    Edinburg, TX 78539

Prairie View A&M University
    Department of
    Communications
    Prairie View, TX 77446

Sam Houston State University
    Journalism Program
    Huntsville, TX 77341

Southern Methodist University
    Center for Communication
    Arts
    Dallas, TX 75275

Southwest Texas State
    University
    Journalism Department
    San Marcos, TX 78666

Stephen F. Austin State
    University
    Department of
    Communications
    Nacogdoches, TX 75962

Texas A&I University
    Department of
    Communications
    Kingsville, TX 78363

Texas A&M University
    Department of
    Journalism
    College Station, TX 77843

Texas Christian University
    Department of Journalism
    Fort Worth, TX 76129

Texas Lutheran College
Department of
Communication
Sequin, TX 78155

Texas Southern University
Department of
Communications
Houston, TX 77004

Texas Tech University
Department of Mass
Communications
Lubbock, TX 79409

Texas Wesleyan College
Department of Mass
Communication
Fort Worth, TX 76105

Texas Woman's University
Department of Journalism
and Broadcasting
Denton, TX 76204

Trinity University
Department of
Communication
San Antonio, TX 78284

University of Houston
School of Communications
Houston, TX 77004

University of Texas
at Arlington
Department of
Communication
Arlington, TX 76019

University of Texas
at Austin
Department of
Journalism
Austin, TX 78712

University of Texas
at El Paso
Department of
Communication
El Paso, TX 79968

University of Texas of the
Permian Basin
Communication Department
Odessa, TX 79762

Utah

Brigham Young University
Department of
Communications
Provo, UT 84602

University of Utah
Department of
Communication
Salt Lake City, UT 84112

Utah State University
  Department of
    Communication
  Logan, UT 84322

Weber State College
  Department of
    Communication
  Ogden, UT 84408

Vermont

St. Michael's College
  Department of Journalism
  Winooski Park, VT 05404

Virginia

Emory and Henry College
  Mass Communications
    Department
  Emory, VA 24327

Hampton University
  Department of Mass Media
    Arts
  Hampton, VA 23668

James Madison University
  Department of
    Communication Arts
  Harrisonburg, VA 22807

Liberty University
  Department of Journalism
  Lynchburg, VA 24506

Mary Baldwin College
  Mass Communications
    Program
  Staunton, VA 24401

Norfolk State University
  Department of Journalism
  Norfolk, VA 23504

Radford University
  Department of
    Communication
  Radford, VA 24142

University of Richmond
  Department of English
  Richmond, VA 23284

Virginia Commonwealth
    University
  School of Mass
    Communication
  Richmond, VA 23284

Virginia Polytechnic Institute
    and State University
  Department of
    Communication
    Studies
  Blacksburg, VA 24061

Virginia Union
University
Department of Journalism
Richmond, VA 23220

Washington and Lee
University
Department of
Journalism and
Communications
Lexington, VA 24450

Washington

Central Washington University
Department of
Communication/
Journalism
Ellensburg, WA 98926

Gonzaga University
Department of
Communication/
Journalism
Spokane, WA 99258

Pacific Lutheran University
Department of
Communication Arts
Tacoma, WA 98447

Seattle University
Journalism Department
Seattle, WA 98122

University of Washington
School of Communications
Seattle, WA 98195

Walla Walla College
Communications
Department
College Place, WA 99324

Washington State University
Department of
Communications
Pullman, WA 99164

Western Washington
University
Department of Journalism
Bellingham, WA 98225

Whitworth College
Department of
Communication Studies
Spokane, WA 99251

West Virginia

Bethany College
Department of
Communication
Bethany, WV 26032

Marshall University
    W. Page Pitt School of
        Journalism
    Huntington, WV 25701

West Virginia University
    Perley Isaac Reed School
        of Journalism
    Morgantown, WV 26506

Wisconsin

Marquette University
    College of Journalism
    Milwaukee, WI 53233

University of Wisconsin

—Eau Claire
    Department of Journalism
    Eau Claire, WI 54701

—La Crosse
    Mass Communications
    La Crosse, WI 54601

—Madison
    School of Journalism and
        Mass Communications
    Department of Agricultural
        Journalism and
    Extension Program in
        Communications
    Madison, WI 53706

—Milwaukee
    Department of Mass
        Communication
    Milwaukee, WI 53201

—Oshkosh
    Department of Journalism
    Oshkosh, WI 54901

—River Falls
    Department of Journalism
    River Falls, WI 54022

—Stevens Point
    Division of Communication
    Stevens Point, WI 54481

—Whitewater
    Mass Communications
        Program
    Whitewater, WI 53190

Wyoming

University of Wyoming
    Department of
        Communications and
        Mass Media
    Laramie, WY 82071

Canada

Carleton University
  School of Journalism
  Ottawa, ON KIS 5B6

Concordia College
  Department of Journalism
  7141 Sherbrooke St. W.
  Montreal, Quebec
  H4B-1R6

Ryerson Polytechnical Institute
  Canada School of
    Journalism
  Toronto, ON M5B 1EB

St. Clair College of
    Applied Arts and
    Technology
  Journalism Department
  Windsor, ON N9A 6S4

University of Calgary
  Communication Studies
    Programme
  Calgary, AL T2N 1N4

University of King's College
  School of Journalism
  Halifax, Nova Scotia
  B3H-4J2

University of Regina
  School of Journalism and
    Communications
  Regina, SK S4S 0A2

University of Western Ontario
  Graduate School of
    Journalism
  London, ON N6A 5B7

University of Windsor
  Department of
    Communication Studies
  Windsor, ON N9B 3P4

SELECTING THE RIGHT COLLEGE FOR YOU

If you plan to study journalism (often referred to in colleges as mass communications), you will want to select your college carefully. Generally, attending colleges with programs accredited by the Accrediting Council on Education in Journalism and Mass Communications will assure the proper balance between journalism classes and other academic programs. However, there are a number of excellent programs offered by institutions that have not applied for the accreditation process. The important element is that the program you take offers only about 25 percent (thirty credits or about ten classes) of your courses in journalism. Naturally, you may want to take more journalism courses, but not at the expense of the rest of your educational program. Graduate with at least ninety credits in other classes.

The Dow Jones Newspaper Fund Journalism and Mass Communications College Search can help you examine colleges. Their service, which helps match your profile of interests with colleges and universities, costs $5. Write for a copy of their career booklet containing an application form. It provides valuable information from one of the most respected organizations promoting excellence in journalism education:

>The Dow Jones Newspaper Fund
>Post Office Box 300
>Princeton, N.J. 08543-0300

GUIDELINES FOR JOURNALISTIC CONDUCT

In a number of places in this book you have seen references to ethics and professional standards. Media take extensive efforts to remind their employees of the important role they play and the need for maintaining standards of conduct. The following is reprinted with permission from *The Arizona Republic, Phoenix Gazette,* and *Arizona Business Gazette.* Jim Patten, coauthor of this book, has provided writing coaching services for these publications. He assisted in the preparation of the following statement on conduct by professional journalists. It is reprinted here as an example of the working conditions for journalists. Similar statements exist in other media and public relations and advertising.

GOALS FOR EXCELLENCE

Introduction

All employees must seek the highest journalistic standards. This statement reinforces those standards and provides goals for professional conduct.

The newspapers' most valuable asset is their credibility. Many elements are involved in winning and keeping our readers' trust. None is more important than accuracy. When we determine we have published inaccurate information, we run prompt corrections.

Fairness, neutrality, objectivity and balance in the news columns are our aim. No one shall be favored or disfavored on our news pages for reasons of race, age, politics, sexual preference, economic status, religion, gender or national origin.

As guests in our readers' homes, we must seek to hold high standards of decency. We bring to our relationship with our readers a sense of courtesy, responsibility and community.

The First Amendment to the Constitution does not belong to us. It belongs to all people. It is our role to defend the First Amendment on their behalf. We resist attempts to weaken or destroy it, no matter what their origin. We accept the obligations imposed upon us by the special privilege of the First Amendment. We recognize that our role includes that of providing a forum for opposing viewpoints.

No statement can, or should, cover all possibilities. Good judgment and professionalism are assumed.

In any case in which the appropriate course is unclear, staff members should seek guidance of their immediate supervisor. Supervisors, in turn, should consult the managing editor or his or her representative before any exception is made.

The publisher and the managing editors have special responsibilities to make exceptions to any suggested guidelines contained here and then only if such exceptions are in the best interests of our readers and of the newspapers.

''Senior Editor'' in this document refers to the publisher, the managing editors, the editors of the editorial pages, the *Arizona Business Gazette* editor, the director of news/editorial resources or their delegated representatives.

General Guidelines

These newspapers depend on teamwork and cooperation from everyone. Employees should treat each other with professional and personal courtesy and respect.

Conscious use of another's writing product, photos or artwork without credit to that person or publication is cause for dismissal. The statement recognizes the possibility of minor use of another's work, as in information gathered from the electronic clip file or databases.

Generally, employees are permitted to appear on radio and television. In their remarks, however, they are encouraged to remain as neutral and objective as they would in newsgathering. Columnists and editorial writers may express judicious opinions. TV and radio appearances, either one-time or regular, must be approved by a senior editor.

Employees are not to use their positions at the newspaper for personal advantage. Employees should make clear their affiliation with the newspapers while engaged in newsgathering. They are not to use the fact of their employment at the newspapers to gain leverage in any situation not involving the newspapers.

Republic, Gazette or *Arizona Business Gazette* stationery should be used exclusively for business.

Staff members may have access to confidential information, news or advertising not known to the public. No employee may take advantage of this information for personal gain.

Staff members should avoid making news decisions about corporations or businesses in which they hold significant ownership interests, such as stock.

News employees should not seek political office or work either in a paid position or as a volunteer for any political campaign, whether for a candidate or ballot issue. Staff members also should not display on their automobiles or in their newsroom bumper stickers, posters, signs or any other material advancing political or social causes. Staff members should avoid attending banquets, dinners, rallies, protests or similar events where their presence might be interpreted as support.

Employees are encouraged to join and take leadership roles in professional journalistic organizations. They should refrain from membership, both advisory and policy-making, in any organization that might be the subject of news coverage.

These newspapers correct errors promptly, clearly and willingly. All corrections must be reviewed by the managing editor or his or her representative.

Free-lance work is permitted only for publications not in direct competition with the newspapers. Supervisors must be informed by staff members before they undertake such work.

No outside employment may be accepted that would cause a conflict of interest or give the appearance of doing so.

With obvious exceptions such as free-lance writers, wire services, etc., we do not pay for news. Analysis or opinions not on the editorial pages must be labeled clearly.

We seek to present the news in a calm, orderly way. Our goal is to transmit information in an interesting but not sensational fashion. Vulgar or obscene words or phrases are limited to quotes and must be justified as essential to the story. Questions about taste should be referred to a supervisor.

The newspapers recognize the rare instance in which an entire story is based upon a confidential source and acknowledge the need to protect such sources. No such sources may be used except when the public has an overriding interest in the material and there is no other way to get it. A senior editor must know the source's identity. The reason such a source is being used must be explained in the story. In the case of wire stories based solely on confidential sources, the news editor on duty must approve their use. The use of confidential sources merely to enhance or add perspective or information to an otherwise attributed story is acceptable, but the reader should be given as much information as possible about the source; for example, "a leading GOP legislator" instead of "a source."

We respect the privacy of innocent people who find themselves in newsworthy situations. While our first goal is to gather and report the news, we do so with sensitivity.

The same standards of decency and fair play that the newspapers require of all other materials apply as well to page layout, headlines, photography, captions and artwork. Headlines and captions must accurately reflect the story or photo they describe. Photographers should not take "set up" news photos. Captions with such photos should not describe actions that did not take place. Retouching of photographs that distorts reality is prohibited.

We treat both genders alike. We do not describe a woman's physical appearance or clothing if we would not do so about a man in a similar context. References to marital status when not germane to the story should be eliminated. We do not use the pronouns "he" or "she" to refer to all members of the human race. Generally, it is best to make the subject plural and use "they" as the pronoun as opposed to a he/she construction.

Tickets, Meals, Gifts, Travel

The newspapers pay their own way.

Free tickets or passes to public events such as movies, recitals, home shows, plays, fairs, circuses, concerts and sports events, where admission is being charged for the public, may not be accepted, solicited or used by employees.

Working press passes or tickets for employees covering the events mentioned above may be accepted. Employees not covering the events but who legitimately need to be there for background purposes also may accept working press passes or tickets. Press passes or tickets may never be given away or sold. Normal use of press facilities, such as sports press boxes, is permitted.

If an organization sends free tickets to the newspapers for general staff use, the tickets should be sent back with a polite explanation of our policies.

As a general rule, employees should not accept free food or drinks from sources or others encountered professionally.

It is acceptable to permit a source to buy a staff member lunch or a drink if the staff expects to have an opportunity to return the favor.

In working situations where food is served, such as at sports events or in hospitality rooms, where staffers would find it awkward either to pay or to refuse to eat, they are permitted to accept their host's hospitality in moderation.

The newspapers discourage alcohol use during working hours, including meals and especially meals with sources. This does not apply to casual, personal encounters with sources.

Books, records, tapes or similar materials sent to the newspapers are to be considered news releases, and they become our property. Such materials, once reviewed, may be kept by the reviewer. Such material not reviewed may be kept by the newspapers for their general use.

We accept no gifts offered because of our employment or position. Gifts must be returned with a polite explanation of our policy. Where this is awkward or impossible, the gifts should be given to charity.

The newspapers pay the travel expenses of their employees on assignment. The newspapers pay the shared costs of staff members who travel on sports team or political candidate planes, trains or busses or any other form of transportation. Staff members may exercise their own judgment in accepting travel in emergency situations, with the understanding that payment will be offered. This policy may be suspended, where necessary and with the permission of senior editors, in the case of stories prepared for travel sections. If a travel writer accepts a free trip, lodging or other hospitality of a host or source, that fact must be prominently and clearly displayed with the resulting story.